Narcissistic Abuse Recovery

How to Heal from Emotional Abuse, Spot Narcissists, and Get Past Abusive Relationships (2022 Guide for Beginners)

Shana Elliott

TABLE OF CONTENTS

Introduction..1

Chapter 1...3

Understanding the Narcissist,..3

Chapter 2..17

An Empath's Relationship with a Narcissist.............................17

Chapter 3..30

The Gaslighting Narcissist,..30

Chapter 4..48

Relationship Narcissism..48

Chapter 5..63

Handling the Narcissist,...63

Chapter 6..86

Women's Fantasies Make Them Easy Prey..................................86

Chapter 7..93

Narcissism in Society,...93

What Are the Characteristics of Narcissistic Leaders?. 103

Chapter 8..109

The Long-Term Effects of Narcissistic Abuse 109

Chapter 9..124

The Seven Steps to Recovery................................124

Conclusion 132

INTRODUCTION

You may have come into contact with a narcissist in your life and sought to learn more about the individual There is a lot of information about Narcissism that can be found everywhere. However, some of it is based solely on assumptions. You may have come across references to narcissists being described as people who are obsessed with themselves and have an exaggerated demand for attention This is correct. Narcissists are always bragging about their appearance, accomplishments, and possessions. They are constantly filled with self-pity.

Narcissism manifests itself in a wide range of behaviors. Individuals with narcissistic personality disorder frequently exhibit a variety of behaviors. Some people are quite self-centered behaviors while others continue to play the victim. The degree of narcissism varies from person to person.

Some people exhibit full-blown narcissism, while others only exhibit a few narcissistic tendencies. You must also understand that not everyone who seeks admiration or plays the victim is a narcissist.

Chapter 1

UNDERSTANDING THE NARCISSIST,

DEFINITION OF NARCISSISM

Narcissism is based on a myth in which a young Greek man named Narcissus fell in love with an image of himself. The story goes as follows:

Narcissus was the river god's son. He was unlike anything else in the world in terms of beauty. Narcissus developed some pride as a result of his beauty and demanded that others adore him as a result of his beauty.

When he went to drink in a pool one day, he noticed a reflection of himself in the still waters. This was my first time seeing it. Narcissus was so taken with what he saw that he couldn't take his gaze away from his reflection.

When he tried to drink from the pool, the still water turned into a ripple, and he couldn't see his reflection. He kept staring into the waters without taking it because he didn't want to lose the beautiful sight of his reflection. Narcissus eventually died of thirst.

In the spot where he died, a lovely flower grew. The flower head was always bent in the same way that Narcissus bowed his head to admire his reflection.

This myth is used to characterize all narcissists. It reveals a hidden reality about narcissists that most people are unaware of.

Narcissus was not smitten by the type of person he was. He was only in love with his reflection in the water. There is a significant distinction between falling in love with oneself and falling in love with an image. Narcissists do not show their true personalities to the public. They present a false image to the world to gain attention and admiration. The image is not of a good person, but someone self-centered and proud of every accomplishment.

When a narcissist is ignored, he or she will continue to complain about being isolated or degraded. Most narcissists are never happy with how others treat them. Their ego is constantly inflated. They rely on their achievements, skills, and the phony image they present to win the hearts of many people. Some make use of their good looks, while others make use of their positions and level of influence. A narcissist believes he or she is superior to everyone else. Such a person will treat others with contempt and maintain his sense of importance.

Narcissists survive on the admiration and praise they receive from others. They are irritated when others criticize or correct them. They despise being out of the spotlight but thrive when they are at the center of attention. When they are criticized, they tend to defend themselves through rage, insults, or any other ill behavior. Most narcissists are manipulators, employing a variety of techniques to manipulate others. Because of such behaviors society tends to ignore or avoid them.

Because of the negative effects, it has on others, narcissism is considered unhealthy. Although everyone has a certain amount of narcissism. That is to say, all humans enjoy good things and enjoy feeling better about themselves. However, when these levels rise too high, it becomes dangerous. Healthy narcissism has no negative consequences for others. Unhealthy narcissism is frequently characterized by poor behavior that destroys many relationships.

IDENTIFYING A NARCISSIST

It is not difficult to recognize a narcissist. Narcissists can ruin a person's life. Because of the characters they portray, they can turn you into a disgusted individual. The following are some of the common characteristics associated with the disorder:

Self-centeredness - Narcissists believe that everything should revolve around them. They will go to any length to attract the attention of others.

Entitlement - they will make the rules and then break them without question.

Demeaning - a narcissist can become bullish at times. He or she may try to bring you down and demonstrate to others that you are unimportant.

Demanding - they will get what they want in any way that seems possible.

Suspicious - Narcissists are always suspicious of anyone who attempts to be friendly and nice to them.

Perfectionism - Narcissists hold others to high standards and expectations. Some of the expectations are frequently unattainable. They will insist on having things done their way.

Snobs - Because they believe they are superior to others, narcissists avoid people who appear to be capable of challenging their position. They become bored when they do not receive the necessary praise and admiration.

Seeking approval - Narcissists are always looking for ways to be recognized for whatever they do.

They lack empathy and are uninterested in the needs of others. It is always difficult for them to comprehend what you are experiencing as an individual. When they make a mistake, they never apologize.

Narcissists are frequently associated with addictive behaviors.

They seek solace in substances such as drugs and alcohol.

There are various types of narcissism. Whatever type of narcissist you encounter, you will notice that they all struggle with empathy. Empathy is the ability to connect with other people's emotions. Narcissists never show empathy for others. How they feel is more important to them than how others feel.

Even if someone else is in pain, narcissists will alter the situation so that it is all about them. If you face a challenge and seek solace from a narcissist, he will pretend to console you. However, you will soon realize that the entire story has changed and that you are the one consoling him for what happened to you.

Narcissists often claim the success that belongs to others. When you accomplish something, they will constantly remind you that you would not have succeeded without them. They will take credit for assignments in which they did not participate. Some will gaslight and lie to you so that you constantly feel bad about yourself. When they make mistakes, they will look for reasons not to accept responsibility. According to research, many people who develop into full-fledged narcissists have experienced traumatic events in their lives.

They were either raised by a narcissistic parent or grew up in an environment where they were underappreciated. A narcissist's personality can be divided into two layers: the outer layer or image and the inner or core image. The person's outer image is what makes them feel loved and appreciated. It is what gives the person comfort and satisfaction.

A person's true personality is reflected in his core image. It is often hidden, but it is filled with bitterness and regret. Most narcissists never let their true personalities be known to the outside world. The reason for this is that they are afraid to confront their true selves, which are often marked by failure and impossibility. Most narcissists are incapable of dealing with their true image. This helps to explain why some of them have low self-esteem. Some people become depressed when they realize their core image is overpowering their outer image.

Although narcissists have two distinct images, they frequently avoid dealing with this fantasy. There are only a few things people can do to help them deal with the darkness of their true identity. That is why they struggle so much to maintain their external image or identity. To accomplish this, they frequently manipulate family members, spouses, neighbors, and friends. They will cover their tracks as they do this so that you do not suspect them. Only careful observers can discern a narcissist's true personality.

MANAGING A NARCISSIST

It is difficult to deal with narcissism. If you've ever had to deal with one, you know how difficult it is to put up with them. Some of the disorder's major behaviors appear to have no solution. The dedication a narcissist has to preserve his image is unparalleled in the world. You will be hurt if you try to persuade him otherwise.

Here are some things to keep in mind when dealing with a narcissist:

1. NARCISSISM COMES IN MANY FORMS.

As stated earlier in this chapter, narcissism is a broad-spectrum disorder.

Different people will take on different personalities. Depending on how a person behaves, the disorder can be mild or severe. An individual may exhibit some narcissistic characteristics but not have NPD. Individuals with few narcissistic tendencies may need to do nothing about their condition as long as it does not affect others.

Some narcissistic people are extremely successful in their endeavors.

Some have successful careers and wonderful families, but their main challenge is their inflated egos. Others are a complete disaster because they are unable to maintain any relationships and have no notable accomplishments. These are frequently thought to have a narcissistic personality disorders.

Several people with NPD may live productive lives in society. However, a significant number of them find it difficult to integrate into most environments. One major challenge for people suffering from NPD is that they never come to terms with the fact that something is wrong with their lives. They will blame the environment and other people for their current situation. Regardless of how bad their situation is, it is nearly impossible to persuade them that they require assistance.

2. NARCISSISM IS DIFFICULT TO DETECT.

When you first meet a narcissist, you will perceive him as any other normal person. For example, it is never easy to tell if you are in the early stages of a relationship with a narcissist

This is because narcissists always conceal their true behaviors in the beginning. However, you will be able to determine the type of person you are dealing with over time.

A narcissistic person is always preoccupied with himself or herself. This limits the opportunities to interact with others and form close relationships. When you're in a relationship and your love and attention aren't returned, you're probably dealing with a narcissist. When a narcissist does something, it is for his satisfaction, not the satisfaction of another person. Narcissists are known to exploit others because they believe they are entitled to everything good that happens around them. They will direct the course of relationships and never treat the other person with the respect he or she deserves.

Such indicators are nearly impossible to detect at the start of a relationship. Narcissistic tendencies do not appear at the start of a relationship. They always appear later, when it is nearly impossible to complete tasks.

Another factor that makes it difficult to identify a narcissist from the start is that most of them appear lovely at first. That explains why some of them get the best jobs in the business. They always interview well and rarely show their flaws at this stage.

A narcissist can easily adapt to a situation by assuming a character that is not his. Narcissists will go to any length to achieve their objectives. Even psychiatrists may take time to correctly diagnose a patient with a narcissistic personality disorder.

Once you've gotten to know someone, you can tell if they're narcissistic if:

The individual continues to think and speak highly of himself or herself.

He believes he can never make a mistake.

He believes he is perfect.

When he has done something wrong, he defends himself.

3. SOME PEOPLE ARE EXTREMELY MANIPULATIVE.

One way to spot a narcissist is through his manipulative behavior. If you get into a relationship with a narcissist, you might notice some strange behaviors over time. Some narcissists find it difficult to express their emotions to their partners. This frequently leads to stressful situations for them. When they are distressed, they will withdraw from friends and family. They find it difficult to share their difficulties with others because they believe they are superior to everyone else.

These kinds of relationships are always one-sided. You will be the one who lavishes the narcissist with love and admiration while receiving nothing in return. Narcissists will only contribute to a relationship if they expect something more in return. Their relationships are frequently shallow and devoid of affection. Narcissists frequently make excuses for not being intimate with their spouses and constantly point out flaws in their partners.

4. NARCISSISTS EXCEL AT GASLIGHTING.

A narcissist will elevate himself by instilling doubt in you.

Narcissists constantly make others doubt their abilities, worth, and strengths. They work hard to make you rely on them more so that they can easily manipulate you. As a result, you are vulnerable and will always agree to their schemes.

Allowing a narcissist to win an argument will keep you from becoming a victim of this type of manipulation. You must understand that persuading a narcissist to buy your idea will be difficult. As a result, you don't need to win a case against them because you'll be frustrated by their tactics. Learn to value yourself. Understand that your success is unrelated to the narcissist and that any negative comments made about you should be ignored.

5. NARCISSISTS CAN PUBLICLY HUMILIATE YOU.

When dealing with a narcissist, it is critical not to offend the person in public. Narcissists are masters of the habit of shaming people in public to make them look good in front of others The narcissist would want to appear mature in a conversation while treating others as children. Narcissists can talk down to you, call you names, and treat you as if you are worthless in front of a crowd so that you will not challenge them. Such actions may give the impression that the narcissist is more mature than you.

Responding to such actions will never improve your situation when dealing with a narcissist. That is why the majority of people avoid arguing with or confronting narcissists in public. If this occurs, simply walk away without saying anything. Attempting to defend yourself may exacerbate the situation.

6. NARCISSISTS CAN CHANGE THE SUBJECT OF A CONVERSATION.

When a conversation does not go in the narcissist's favor, he or she may change the subject to avoid any irresponsibility. When others are in the middle of a conversation, narcissists are known to change the subject. They frequently do this when the focus has shifted from them to someone else. Many of them do this to avoid taking responsibility or accountability for their failures. Diverting the conversation is also a good way to bring the group's attention back to them.

When this happens, conversations will end with no solid outcome. Many issues will also go unresolved, and no errors will be corrected.

7. NARCISSISTS ALWAYS AVOID CONFRONTING THE REAL ISSUE.

Triangulation is a skill that narcissists excel at. They will include third parties in their argument to appear credible. They will always call someone to testify as their witness to dismiss any accusations leveled against them. This is frequently done to win an argument, even if they are incorrect.

The witness is always someone who admires or trusts the narcissist. They may also involve someone who appears to be a threat to the victim. For example, your current partner may have your ex-partner testify against you. The narcissistic partner will then force you to submit to their demands.

A narcissist may also project your words and thoughts to others rather than keeping them between the two of you. Projection can happen in a variety of ways. There is one type that appears to be a compliment but is not. Narcissists constantly use projection to abuse their victims. They may also use it to conceal their flaws and to force you to admit mistakes on their behalf.

8. NARCISSISTS ARE GOOD AT CALLING PEOPLE NAMES.

When dealing with a narcissist, be prepared to hear hurtful words. Narcissists are masters of epithets. They use insults to outwit and manipulate their opponents into submission. When you are insulted by a narcissist, it is best not to respond in kind. This will make you appear more mature and emotionally in control.

A narcissist may insult you for no reason at all. Particularly if you pose a threat to his position. Some narcissists do this because they have been bullied in the past. If you let their insults get to you, you may develop low self-esteem and begin to look down on yourself. It is critical that you do not take these insults personally.

The majority of narcissists never seek help. They will never admit that they require therapy. Instead, they will continue to rely on others to meet their needs. It takes a trained professional to make a narcissist see his flaws. When dealing with a narcissistic partner, it is sometimes best to end the relationship. This is only advised if the relationship is negatively impacting your psychological, mental, and physical health.

Chapter 2

AN EMPATH'S RELATIONSHIP WITH A NARCISSIST

You must be able to tell whether you are an empath or a narcissist as an individual. An empath is someone who prioritizes the needs of others over his own. Empathic people are often preoccupied with helping others. A narcissist prioritizes his own needs. Narcissists frequently use their interests to motivate themselves.

Empaths and narcissists have one thing in common: their intelligence level. Empaths have a high level of affective empathy, whereas narcissists have a high level of cognitive empathy. Narcissists can recognize how others think to manipulate them. Empaths frequently detect and respond to the emotions of others. This shows that empaths and narcissists can both understand the needs, motivations, and desires of others. What distinguishes them is how they respond to these needs.

Empaths benefit from other people's emotions, whereas narcissists exploit them for personal gain. An empathic person will take your problem and make it their own while looking for a solution. A narcissist will exploit others' frustrations by manipulating their emotions.

Surprisingly, empaths and narcissists are frequently attracted to each other. Empaths are always motivated when they help others.

Narcissists are wounded people who want to be helped in any way they can. Because empaths find fulfillment in assisting those who are suffering, they are prone to suffering greatly themselves.

WHY DO NARCISSISTS AND EMPATHS GET ALONG?

Narcissists and empaths frequently get along because narcissists can easily meet their narcissistic supply by empaths' desire to help them. In the majority of cases, narcissistic men marry empaths as wives. These women frequently wonder what is wrong with them.

Narcissists are constantly frustrated by their way of life. They tend to seek fulfillment where which is how they end up associating with empaths. Because narcissists are constantly seeking attention, they require constant affirmation and assurance, which fellow narcissists are unable to provide. Even when they meet empathic people, it is difficult to please them due to their constantly shifting demands and goalposts. As a result, such relationships are unlikely to last because the empathic person grows tired of giving attention while receiving nothing in return. In a nutshell, here are some of the reasons why narcissists and empaths are often attracted to one another.

They are mirror images of one another. A narcissist requires constant attention. An empath requires a place to be kind.

Empaths and narcissists are prone to projecting their frustrations and fears onto one another. Empaths are afraid of being rejected, while narcissists are afraid of being vulnerable.

Individuals who have not matured in their empathetic skills frequently engage in relationships with narcissists because they do not understand what it is like to be manipulated. They always find fulfillment in loving others while putting themselves last. Because they don't know how to set boundaries when it comes to acts of kindness, they always rely on narcissists to do so. Because they are unable to disconnect from their emotions, such people find it difficult to form healthy relationships.

Narcissists are always dependent on empaths. They have no idea how to deal with their emotions. As a result, they rely on empaths to make emotional decisions. Narcissists are the condition that is always present at birth. It is their life circumstances that cause them to develop narcissistic tendencies. They frequently lose their sense of connecting with other people's emotions as they gain experience. They consider empathy to be a sign of weakness. That is why they try as hard as they can not be kind to anyone.

There must be a sense of balance between an empath and a narcissist for them to survive in a relationship. There will be healthy relationships if an empath can detect any form of abuse and set boundaries against it. If an empath, for example, abandons a narcissist and refuses to bow to his demands, the narcissist will be left with no one to project his emotions onto. This can help the narcissist deal with his emotions more effectively. However, if the narcissist does not realize his error, he will simply move on to the next victim. Moving to a place where people can handle and manage their emotions is the solution to healing.

Each individual must recognize their dark side and be able to control the negative emotions associated with their personality. When this is accomplished, empaths and narcissists can easily collaborate to build a healthy society. In any case, it is the empath who suffers the most from an unhealthy relationship with a narcissist. Although empaths derive their energy from assisting others, it can be exhausting at times. Here are some strategies empaths can use to stay in a relationship with a narcissist.

1. Concentrate on yourself – As an empath, it is always a good idea to focus on yourself as you seek to help others.

Remember that you must maintain emotional stability to stand with others. What you don't have, you can't give to the world. If your emotions are out of control, you may struggle to complete your assignment of assisting others. Keep your needs in mind. Spend time caring for your mind, body, and emotions. This is beneficial to you.

2. Rest – When you are feeling overwhelmed, it is critical that you take a break from the relationship to reflect and rest. When your emotions are depleted, you may feel weak when others require you. It is critical to take some time to recharge your batteries. You can spend time walking or doing activities that you enjoy to clear your mind.

3. Meditate – Meditation allows you to control your emotions and heal from any negative experiences. Begin with a few minutes of meditation each day and gradually increase the time. This increases your awareness of what is going on around you. If you have a narcissist in your life, meditation can help you restore your memory and avoid any form of manipulation.

4. Protect yourself – empaths are prone to quickly copying the negative energy of others. If you anticipate that your narcissistic partner will derail your focus, you can devise strategies to protect yourself. You may form a protective

bubble around your thoughts or actions to keep out any form of abuse.

5. Seek out a mentor - Counsellors and other mentors can also assist you in dealing with a difficult spouse. As an empath, your role will always revolve around meeting your spouse's emotional needs. This means you'll need people to motivate you to get through some of the difficult situations that a narcissistic spouse will put you through.

If a narcissist realizes you have a problem with your compassionate nature, he or she may take advantage of you, and you may end up focusing more on them. As you try to please your spouse, you may completely forget about yourself.

Determine who will be there for you in times of need. One with whom you can talk about your problems and who will support you when you are struggling with your own emotions.

Remember that no matter how strong you are, there are some things you simply cannot overcome on your own.

6. Prioritize your time - When you have the energy, it is critical to prioritize the needs of others and how you will meet them. Remember that, in addition to your spouse, there may be others who look to you for support. If you spend everything,

Your time spent meeting your spouse's narcissistic nature may result in the loss of some good relationships.

Set your priorities correctly. Don't expend all of your energy helping others. You will notice that more and more people will approach you for assistance, but you must know when to work and when to rest. Apart from your partner, identify other people who value your assistance and continue to provide it to them.

7. Follow your dreams - Empaths are often so focused on meeting the needs of their narcissistic spouses that they forget to follow their own. Spend more time pursuing your goals, desires, and ambitions now and then, rather than focusing on achieving them.

Spend some time developing your vision and striking a balance between serving others and pursuing your dream.

When dealing with narcissists, empaths require a lot of advice. This is because narcissists tend to take advantage of the type of assistance they receive from empathic spouses. Although it is beneficial to connect with the emotions of others, you must recognize that you must also take care of yourself. You can easily grow your relationship to a healthy one by following the tips outlined above and setting an example for others. The ultimate goal is that you pursue your life goals while remaining safe and comfortable.

As an empath, you must also recognize that you cannot meet all of your spouse's needs. You must therefore be careful not to become completely immersed in your spouse's emotions or to lose sight of your own needs.

You should also understand that being in a relationship with a narcissist is difficult. You must confront and understand your demons. There will be times when you will feel compelled to assist your spouse. However, you must do so in moderation so that you do not exhaust all of your energy. Make a note of your issues and resolve them as soon as possible to avoid getting into a bind while attempting to help others.

Feeling obligated to your spouse's emotions is something you will continue to feel. However, you must first attempt to work on yourself.

IF YOU DON'T, YOU MIGHT END UP HURTING THE PEOPLE YOU'RE TRYING TO HELP.

Toxic attractions frequently end in disaster. Because of their kind heart and sense of giving, narcissists frequently seek out empaths. They are aware that they will have someone to manipulate to satisfy their need for attention. Unfortunately, empaths are not drawn to narcissists because of who they are.

Instead, they are drawn to the narcissist's image of a perfect individual ready to build a solid relationship. A narcissist's first impression is frequently false. When you first meet a narcissist, you will perceive him or her to be intelligent, responsible, and charming. When you stop meeting their demands, you will see the other side of their personality.

If you are an empath and do not meet the demands of your narcissistic spouse, you will always face cold treatment and punishment. When the narcissist is around other people, he may appear to be very nice and loving, but when it comes to you, things may be different.

Some narcissists enter relationships with empaths expecting them to change. For some, this is the norm, while for others, things worsen. This is because narcissists are always focused on themselves and may never see anything positive in their spouse. They always blame their spouses for their flaws and may manipulate them to appear in command.

When dealing with a narcissistic spouse, keep in mind that it may take some time for them to reveal their true identity.

Although most people are advised to avoid narcissistic people when choosing a spouse, a large number of empaths end up in their arms without their knowledge. During the early days of their marriage, these two always seem to get along. The narcissist frequently constructs a temporary pedestal for the individual. With things begin to change over time, and because most empaths believe they can heal any heart through compassion, they choose to fight for such unions until they can no longer bear the pain.

NARCISSISTS ENJOY CHAOS, DRAMA, AND DISAGREEMENTS.

Empaths, on the other hand, always prioritize peace and healthy relationships. Narcissists do not thrive in peaceful settings.

They enjoy it when people disagree with them. They can easily manipulate others into destroying the peace that exists between them. They always act as victims in front of their spouses, taking advantage of any form of kindness that comes their way.

Empaths always treat everyone equally because they believe that every human being deserves to be treated with compassion. They are always willing to help others realize their vision. They want to see others grow.

As a result, they always maintain a high level of patience when interacting with people who are not as sympathetic. Narcissists frequently use this to exert control over their spouses. Because empaths are needed to support others, the narcissist ends up exploiting them for his interests and gain.

THE EMPATH AND THE TRAUMA BOND

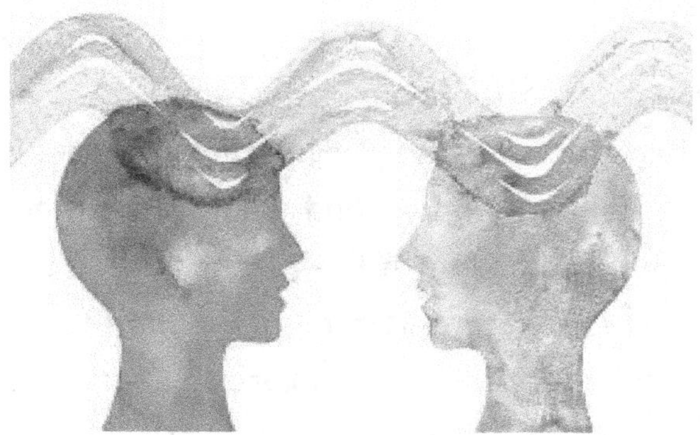

Because of their manipulative nature, narcissists frequently form bonds with empaths. This is referred to as the trauma bond.

That is why it is always impossible for an empath to leave an abusive relationship. In most cases, the empath does not see herself as the victim; instead, he treats the narcissist as the victim and tries to help as much as he can.

Individuals can use empathy to reflect on their actions, identify flaws, and make necessary changes. During the trauma bond, the compassionate spouse will reflect on their mistakes and make the necessary changes. This will not be the case for the narcissist. A narcissist will blame the empath for everything and use their ability to apologize to further manipulate them. This creates a cycle in which the narcissist makes a mistake, blames the empath, and the empath looks for ways to improve on their mistakes.

It is never easy for empaths to admit they are in a toxic relationship with a narcissist. However, as an empath, you should always be on the lookout for some of the red flags associated with narcissistic relationships to protect yourself from any form of trauma.

When you accept that you are dating or married to a narcissist, it becomes much easier to protect yourself from any form of abuse. You will understand what to do to ensure that you are growing in addition to the relationship. You will also understand how to treat those around you so that you do not lose them to gaslighting. You must exercise caution so that you do not end up doing all of your spouse's work.

You must also understand that boundaries are necessary to survive such a relationship. Empaths make every effort to operate without boundaries. They must, however, understand when to agree to demand and when to refuse it. You must make certain that your generosity is not exploited.

Most empaths are often soft-hearted; they rarely recognize their independence. However, you must know when to hold on to a relationship and when to let it go.

THE EMPATH AND THE HEALING IDEA

Empathetic people have the unique ability to identify the pains of others and embrace the pain as if it were their own.

When attempting to correct the narcissist's flaws, a large number of them become attracted to the narcissist.

Most of the time, the empath is unaware that the narcissist is only there to take. He can drain your energy, as well as your sanity and emotions. Although it is admirable to help others, most empaths end up in trouble, especially if they do not understand the importance of setting boundaries.

In most narcissist-empath relationships, the empath is perplexed by the entire situation. The reason for this is that the narcissist may never recognize her value and assistance. An empath, on the other hand, will always put himself in the shoes of the narcissist and connect with his feelings. He or she will do so without being aware of the narcissistic agenda.

In a nutshell, empath-narcissist relationships will always work. The difficulty arises when neither of them addresses their emotional instabilities. If the narcissist's agenda is still being manipulated, the relationship may not grow properly, even if the empath is working hard to build it. Even if the empath wants to love and care for the narcissist, things may not work out if there is no balance. Indeed, as the empath grows in love, the narcissist becomes more demanding and controlling.

As the narcissist gains power, the empath may withdraw and play the victim. As a result, the empath may begin to exhibit narcissistic traits to retaliate against their spouse's bad behavior. The relationship will soon come to an end.

When narcissistic spouse learns that their partner has been injured, they will use it to cause even more pain. A narcissist enjoys superiority more as an empath drowns in their pain. The empath may begin to seek love and approval elsewhere, and this is how an affair enters the relationship.

Although empaths and narcissists are always attracted to each other, the relationship frequently ends in frustration. As a result, many empaths nowadays avoid narcissists as partners. When a relationship is new, a narcissist does not appear to be a threat to an empath. However, as time passes, it becomes clear that an empath's strengths pose a threat to the narcissist, resulting in numerous conflicts.

Chapter 3

THE GASLIGHTING NARCISSIST,

One type of emotional abuse is gaslighting. A gas lighter is someone who makes you doubt what is true. Such a person will try to erase your memory of an action or event by bombarding your mind with ideas and thoughts that are opposed to reality. Gas lighters frequently succeed in convincing you that your beliefs are merely figments of your imagination. Their goal is to alter your perception of them and your surroundings.

Gaslighting is an abusive strategy that causes you to doubt your feelings and thoughts. A gaslighter, for example, will make you believe that whatever you are saying is not true while you are communicating. The person may dismiss all of your efforts to appear good in front of others. A gas lighter will cause you to doubt your intelligence, memory, and abilities. You may try to argue about it, but you will eventually give up and begin to doubt yourself.

When you are a victim of gaslighting, you may lose faith in your emotions. As a result, you'll have to rely on the gas lighter to approve anything you say. When you give the abuser your trust, he will take advantage of the situation to manipulate you. Most people consider gaslighting to be emotional abuse. It is frequently associated with men rather than women. Although gaslighting is common in romantic relationships, it can occur in any setting, including the workplace.

There are various types of gaslighting. It can be either emotional, verbal, or done without the victim's knowledge. Among the most common gaslighting techniques are:

Denial – The gas lighter may also pretend to have forgotten anything related to a specific occurrence. When they do so,

You will begin to doubt your memory. When such a person makes such promises to you, he may completely deny ever saying anything of the sort, making you look foolish.

Withholding occurs when the gas lighter completely disregards your concerns. Even if you have told them about your problem, the person can pretend that he or she was unaware of it.

Gas lighters are also adept at changing the subject of conversation. They do this to avoid answering any questions about themselves. For example, you may start a conversation with a gas lighter only to have it devolve into a conflict because the gas lighter begins to doubt the credibility of any detail you provide.

Countering is when the gas lighter questions your ability to remember things. You may have witnessed an incident involving the individual. But he will completely deny it and twist every detail of the event to confuse you.

A gas lighter may treat you poorly if you are trivialized. He may accuse you of overreacting if you react to such treatment. This can lead you to believe that you are the weak one and that the gas lighter is emotionally stronger.

Gas lighters will always closely monitor your conversations to detect any errors. They will exploit such errors to play the victim.

A gaslighting narcissist, for example, may insult and accuse you when you react to the action. In such a case, you may be forced to apologize, even though you are the victim.

Gaslighting narcissists always use manipulation to maintain power. Their goal is to destabilize your perception of reality and deceive you into believing you have brain fog. They distort all of your memories to abuse your personality. When a narcissist employs gaslighting on you, he or she will make derogatory remarks that test your intellectual capacity. They may cause others to question your sanity. Nobody will ever believe your actions, perceptions, or ideas.

Gaslighting can cause you to lose your ability to stand up for the truth. Narcissistic gaslighters can sabotage your in every way your activities and force you to rely on them for validation. You may believe you have a mental illness if you have such a person as a friend, colleague, or partner.

Gaslighting is more common in malignant narcissists because they use it to avoid acknowledging their emotional and psychological abuse. Such people lack the moral fortitude to admit their mistakes. They can annoy you to the point where you have to rely on them for every decision you make.

A gaslighting narcissist is essentially a target for severe trauma. If you have such a person as a spouse or close relative, you may suffer greatly as a result of the incorrect perception you will develop in yourself and others. A gaslighting narcissist can do the following to you:

1. CHANGING YOUR ATTITUDE TOWARD OTHERS

Before befriending someone, you tend to believe that they are good. However, if you experience trauma at the hands of those who are supposed to protect you, you will develop a different perception of them. Some people face difficulties and pain when they are young. The perception caused by this pain sticks with them as they grow. If you end up in a relationship with a gaslighting narcissist, you may confirm your fears, which can be difficult to change.

For example, if you are in a relationship with a narcissist, you may be convinced that he or she is a wonderful person. After a while, you realize that the person you thought was good has turned into a source of pain and misery. Such a reality can be extremely traumatic, especially if you have previously encountered a narcissist. This can give you a broad perspective on other people. As a result, you may find it difficult to interact with others, no matter how nice they appear to be.

2. MAKING YOU DOUBT YOURSELF

Gaslighting narcissists can convince you that you cannot survive without their assistance. That is their goal. Even when you are certain of what you are doing, the gas lighter will keep reminding you how insane you are and what you're saying He will make you rely on him because you will begin to believe that you are unstable.

You become the gas lighter's narcissistic supply as a result, and the person will continue to manipulate you as long as you agree with his demands. Gas lighters can lead you to believe that your perception is incorrect. They can even rearrange your belongings to make you believe you are not responsible enough. They will do everything in their power to convince you that you are insane. Some even go so far as to inform your close relatives and friends that you have a problem, which is not the case.

3. ENDANGERING YOUR RELATIONSHIPS

Splitting is a tactic used by gaslighting narcissists. This is when a gas lighter speaks negatively about others in your presence and tells them negative things about you. By doing so, the gas lighter isolates you from those who would have defended you. Gaslighting narcissists will always make certain that nothing distracts you from their narcissism. They will spread lies about you to your family and friends to keep them away from you.

4. MAKING YOU DISTRUSTFUL OF OTHERS

Narcissists who gaslight are excellent manipulators. For example, if you have a gas lighter for a spouse, he or she may make you jealous by bragging about how good their ex-partners were. Other people may be dying to be in a relationship with such spouses.

As a result, you may begin to distance yourself from certain people, believing that they are out to destroy your relationship. Gaslighting narcissists frequently turns you against others and can isolate you from the people who are important in your life.

Gaslighters can lead to a very lonely and self-doubting life if you are not careful. Because of the information you may have received from the gas lighter, you begin to treat others suspiciously.

5. MAKING YOU FEEL BAD

If you end up in a relationship with a gas lighter, you may come to despise being in a relationship. Gaslighting

At the start of a relationship, narcissists are always charming. They will lavish you with their affection and love. As soon as you begin to trust them, they will begin to mistreat you and reveal their true character.

Most people end up with a gaslighting narcissist as a spouse because the person will treat you as special at the start of the relationship. This makes you believe in him or her and trust in their love. When it appears that it is too late to back down, the person will begin to push you out of thieves and make you believe that you are worthless.

When this occurs and you successfully exit such a relationship, it will take some time for you to consider entering another relationship. You'll always be afraid that something similar will happen in your new relationship.

6. UNDERMINING YOUR IDENTITY

Gaslight narcissists can make you forget who you are.

They can make you doubt your abilities and sap your enthusiasm for certain activities. Even if you have accomplished something wonderful, they will make you believe that you have not given your all. They do this to prevent you from becoming a threat to their position.

7. ISOLATION FROM YOUR CHILDREN

If you marry a gaslighting narcissist, he or she may distort the perception your children form of you. The majority of gas lighters raise their children to be narcissists as well. When it comes to interacting with their children, many of them lack boundaries. When a child begins to distance himself or herself from such a parent, he or she is subjected to a great deal of abuse.

Gaslighting narcissists always expect everyone's loyalty. As a result, their children can never refuse their instructions.

A gaslighting spouse will spread negative information about you to your children.

Most of this information is often false and intended to turn children away from you. Gaslighters use this technique to draw their children's attention to themselves.

NARCISSISTIC GASLIGHTING WARNING SIGNS

Gaslighting is a tactic used by narcissists to gain power over their victims. Most narcissists employ this tactic because it is effective in forcing others to submit to them. One risk of gaslighting is that it occurs in a slow but gradual manner.

You may never suspect anything as a victim until you are completely brainwashed. These are the warning signs that you are engaging in gaslighting narcissism:

1. Lies - Narcissists who gaslight are liars. They will tell and keep a lie. They are not concerned about being caught lying. The majority of them base their manipulation on lies. When you believe their lies, everything else they do or say appears to be true.

2. The use of what is close to you as a manipulative object - because they know what is close to your heart, they will use it to fight your sanity. For example, if they know your children are close to you, they will attack them first. For example, they may begin by telling you that if you want to have a healthy relationship with your children, you must establish a boundary between yourself and them. This may sound like sound advice to you, but it is simply a

means of isolating yourself from the same people who can protect you from the gas lighter.

3. Tiredness – this happens gradually, but the effects accumulate over time. Gas lighters start with a few lies here and there. You will eventually realize that your entire life has revolved around a series of lies. Because gaslighting is frequently disguised as some form of assistance, even the most intelligent people are frequently gaslighted. You eventually realize that you can no longer fend for yourself and that you must rely on the gas lighter to survive.

4. Denial of the truth – even if you have proof that a gas lighter said something, he or she will never admit it. A gas lighter can do or say something one moment and completely change it the next. Even if you have proof of the incident, the gas lighter will always deny ever happening taking part in it When this happens, you will begin to doubt your memory and believe whatever they are claiming to be true.

The more a gas lighter denies reality, the more you doubt your judgment. You will eventually start accepting their opinion as true, and this is how you will fall into the manipulator's trap.

5. Enmity with those close to you – if you notice that people who were once close to you are creating distance, you should suspect that the gas lighter is sabotaging you behind your back. Without your knowledge, a gaslighting narcissist can turn people against you. He can turn people against you by telling them that you are not the type of person they should keep as a friend. They may also turn

you against others by convincing you that others do not value your friendship. They gain more control over your mind and emotions by isolating you.

6. Misalignment of actions and words – Gas lighters frequently do the opposite of what they say. When dealing with a gas lighter, avoid focusing on their words. Instead, concentrate on their actions because their words are always deceptive.

7. Confusion – Gas lighters may occasionally mix sentiments to confuse you. For example, someone may tell you how useless you are right now. The following day, the same person may begin praising you for an accomplishment you have made. This can be perplexing because you may not know which side of the gas lighter to believe. A gas lighter can abuse a child now and then shower the same child with expensive gifts later on.

By doing so, he can erase any negative memories the child may have had of him.

8. Calling you crazy - anyone who constantly reminds you how insane you are could be a gas lighter. This is one of their most common techniques. Gas lighters believe that if you begin to doubt your sanity, you will be unable to persuade others that the gas lighter is abusing you.

Knowing these techniques is important when dealing with a gaslighting narcissist because you will learn how to defend yourself from them Such knowledge can also keep you from becoming enslaved by a narcissist.

GASLIGHTING NARCISSISTS' COMMON PHASES

Aside from the warning signs mentioned above, you should also be aware of the types of phrases to avoid. These phrases are frequently used by narcissists to demean and manipulate their victims into submission. Let us take a look at a few of them:

PHRASE 1: YOU ARE ENVIOUS AND INSECURE.

A gaslighting narcissist will constantly make you envious of others.

They will flood your mind with incidents that will make you feel insecure. They will also make you doubt your abilities and attractiveness. When you question their affairs or questionable activities, you will be told that you are just insecure or jealous.

Gas lighters are naturally deceptive. It is up to you to maintain your composure when they try to manipulate your emotions. Learn how to deal with their business and competitive nature.

A gaslighting narcissist will use triangulation to take control of you. He will instill jealousy in any form, then portray you as a weakling incapable of controlling emotions. When you're in a relationship with someone like this, they may use affairs to make you jealous to make you love them even more.

PHRASE NUMBER TWO: FORGET ABOUT IT.

When you try to bring up a past issue, gaslighting narcissists will make such a statement. They will not give you enough space to recover from abusive situations. They expect you to forget about the incident and move on without bringing it up again.

When you remind gas lighters of their bad behavior, they get angry. They want to keep control, and you should not question it. They always expect you to bury any past experiences that have not been resolved. Nonetheless, they will continue to be abusive. They may pretend to treat you well for a short time to regain your trust. They strike again after you appear to have made progress. It becomes a cycle of abuse, frustration, and a little bit of love. You should be wary of this strategy because it has the potential to harm you.

You stay in an abusive relationship because you are occasionally showered with affection.

A gas lighter can terrorize your life today, then return the next day acting as if nothing happened. They will encourage you to let go of the past so that the cycle can begin again. This is referred to as trauma bonding. You become addicted to an abuser due to the affection you receive from them.

PHRASE 3: YOU ARE ONLY EXAGGERATING.

This phrase will be used by a gaslighting narcissist to demonstrate that you are too sensitive for nothing. This usually occurs when you attempt to respond to their insensitive nature.

This phrase is also intended to convey to you that your emotions as a victim are unimportant. As long as it gives him pleasure, a narcissist will continue to mistreat you. He or she will enjoy dragging you down and causing you pain to keep you under their control.

One of the consequences of gaslighting is that people begin to wonder if they are being overly sensitive all of the time. If you find yourself asking this question repeatedly, you may need to identify the gas lighter in your life.

Claiming that the victim is oversensitive is a common tactic used by malignant narcissists to conceal the need for help in dealing with the abuse. Narcissists who abuse others physically and psychologically tend to convince them that they should never overreact. Once victims believe this, they can suffer in silence for years without seeking assistance. They do this because they have been brainwashed into believing that whatever they are going through is insignificant enough to cause friction between them and the gas lighter.

In reality, no abuse should be tolerated. Even if one chooses to remain silent, the effect is never positive. As a result, abusive narcissists should never be taken lightly. A good person is someone who allows you to express your emotions. This is something that a gaslighting narcissist could never do.

Instead, he will always shift his attention from your emotions to his own.

NO. 4: YOU HAVE MENTAL HEALTH ISSUES THAT REQUIRE TREATMENT.

When a narcissist says this, he simply means that you are the source of the problem. Most narcissists will say this when they realize you're trying to react to their behavior. This will lead you to believe that they do not have a problem.

They shift the blame to you and portray themselves as the victim. If you focus on such statements, you will come to believe that you are the source of the problem. This type of manipulation is frequently difficult to detect. When you believe you are the only one who has a problem, it is difficult to escape the narcissist's abuse.

Narcissistic gas lighters always act as if they have a solution to their victims' problems. They will inform you that you have a problem and will offer to help you. You will accept this offer despite knowing that it is a form of manipulation. The outcomes will be poor. Abusers use this tactic to ensure that you do not report them. They erode your credibility to the point where society no longer believes what you say. They lead people to believe that you are the source of the problem.

NO. 5: YOU APPEAR TO BE THE ISSUE.

Gas lighters are always aware that they are the source of the problem. However, they will never admit it. They will continue to attack you by shifting the goalposts so that you cannot pin them down. They can keep raising their expectations of you until you appear to be accomplishing nothing. This keeps you busy as you try to correct your errors to meet their expectations.

Gaslighting narcissists take comfort in the fact that you will always try to meet their expectations. They will even refer to you as a gas lighter yourself. They can even switch roles and make you act like a narcissist to play the victim.

This will lead you to believe that you are the one with a problem. If you seek outside assistance, they will blame you for their mistakes and accuse you of sabotage.

NO. 6: IT WASN'T SERIOUS.

A narcissist will abuse you but claim it was all in good fun.

gas lighters frequently disguise their abusive behavior as jokes. They will call you derogatory names and humiliate you in public. When you complain, they will tell you that it was all a joke and that you need to learn to value the role of humor in conversations.

Narcissists who have mastered the art of gaslighting can treat you however they want and get away with it because they know you will take it as a joke.

You should be wary of any nasty comments disguised as jokes.

This is an example of verbal abuse that should not be tolerated.

It can sometimes come across as teasing. However, you must be careful to distinguish between the two. If a phrase or comment is intended to harm your reputation, you should take it seriously. gas lighters will demean you and pretend they weren't serious to avoid having to apologize. Their ego will not allow them to do so.

When dealing with a gaslighting narcissist, it is critical that you do not allow yourself to be publicly humiliated. Understand the difference between humor and something more serious. Encouraging such behavior in public can erode your reputation over time. When dealing with such a person, emphasize the importance of boundaries. If you are in a relationship, make sure to establish boundaries early on so that you do not struggle later. Tolerating such behavior early in a relationship may lead to psychological abuse and violence later on.

PHRASE NO. 7: YOU ARE MAKING UP YOUR SCENARIOS.

Such a phrase will cause you to question your belief in the narcissist.

You will begin to doubt the accuracy of your memory of the person. You will begin to believe that you are imagining things and that you no longer have control over your mind. You may begin to believe that you are insane at some point. The narcissist will find every reason to justify your situation.

Most gaslighting victims are unable to distinguish between reality and their imaginations. At the end of the day, they tend to be confused because their thought pattern has been completely eroded.

GETTING RID OF GASLIGHTING

The first step in overcoming a gaslighting narcissist is to recognize that such a person exists. It is easier to find held once you understand the type of manipulation you have been subjected to.

- Here are some suggestions to help you get out of a sticky situation.
- Make no excuses for the bad behavior of others.
- Never give up your feelings for the person.
- Maintain your integrity and resist all forms of manipulation.
- Prioritize your safety.
- Engage a licensed therapist.

Chapter 4

RELATIONSHIP NARCISSISM

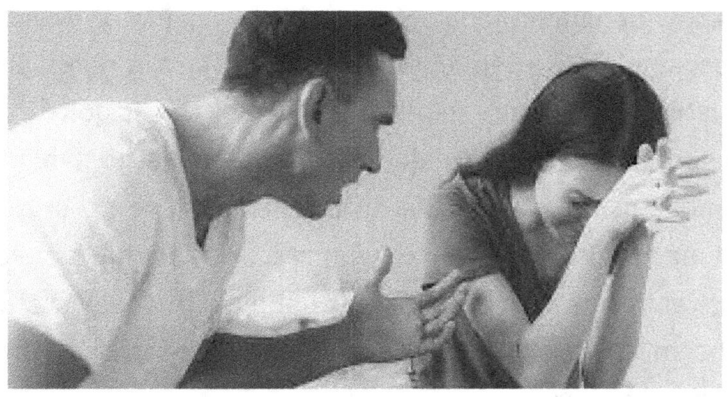

Because of the random nature of humankind, broad generalizations about human characters may be inappropriate. Finding a narcissist requires a keen eye because such people hide their true faces behind humor and empathy. They can easily attract with first impressions such as good looks and conspicuous kindness that anyone can feel. This could, however, be the start of a very stressful relationship, one full of emotional sabotage and deception.

Contrary to popular belief, narcissists can fall in love just like anyone else. In such a case, the true identity of a narcissist emerges gradually over time. The relationship will then become more toxic from time to time, providing a hell of an experience for a partner.

Mistreatment from the narcissistic better half can cause a partner to lose self-esteem. As a result, narcissistic relationships are prone to dissolution.

Some narcissism cannot be hidden, and its toxicity is readily apparent. Individuals in this class are wearing their true faces. They act by their reasoning, so they are as they should be. Against all odds, such people have been seen to be attracted to sensitive people. This may go against the wishes of the person in question, but it is a natural fact in narcissistic relationships. The observation, on the other hand, is quite ironic in how someone will fail to identify the narcissist to avoid bad experiences in a precious life. lives partners are narcissists, and the manifestation of narcissism in a relationship can vary. Another factor is when one partner behaves in a way that can cause harm to his or her better half. The first factor is rarely seen, but it does exist.

When this occurs, partners cannot simply let go for reasons other than true love. The latter is now evident in many cases, as evidenced by the numerous abusive relationships observed among the couples. A narcissist's bad behavior could include being canter-minded, putting his/her needs ahead of the significant needs of the better half.

- Relationship Narcissism Symptoms
- They frequently make one feel guilty.

- They are skilled at manipulation and will frequently try to make you feel defeated and guilty for reasons that they have created.

They have a way of making you feel sorry for things they have done or for trivial reasons. They will blame you for reasons that are entirely their fault; they are also known for looking for minor flaws and making it appear as if you are making a major mistake.

THEY ARE DECEPTIVE.

A narcissist is someone who will overcome any obstacle to obtain what they desire. Such people would want to put you in a position to help them achieve their objectives.

Making you perform roles that you would not have chosen for personal reasons. Such manipulation comes naturally to narcissists because they regard themselves as unique and confident in their abilities.

ENTITLEMENT

The narcissistic disorder appears to give some of its victims a strong belief that they will get what they want. That they can command, and everything they desire will be accomplished through you.

They consider their own needs to be more important than those of their partners and believe that they should be met as soon as possible. Over time, this creates abusive relationships, causing their partners to have dreadful love experiences.

They appear to defy some universal rules.

Because of their sense of self-importance, narcissists act as if certain rules should not apply to them. They are seen to push ahead of their colleagues regardless of public gatherings as if they do not value others. They are also known for standing in this category versus anyone, regardless of rank To boost their esteem, narcissists step on everyone in the way they do things; they believe they are special, and thus their power and control should be validated.

PERSISTENT DANGERS

This is also a true narcissistic trait; it is associated with a short temper. Someone who threatens you with phrases like 'I didn't need you anyway, you can leave me alone is unlikely to be a good long-term partner. The best way to deal with such situations will be discussed later in this article.

EXTERNALLY APPEALING

Narcissists have a common way of making themselves appealing, whether it's through their social lives, possessions, or general physical appearance.

They frequently conceal their true selves, and while they can dazzle onlookers, they are huge social misfits on the inside. This factor is related to the others mentioned above in the sense that most narcissists have a sense of self-importance, making them feel superior to others. They make it appear as if this is a fact by making themselves appear quite impressive. It does not, however, change anything about them.

THEY BELIEVE THEY ARE UNIQUE.

If you believe you cannot live without him or her, you may be in a relationship with a narcissist. When compared to others, narcissists place a high value on their specialization. Such individuals believe that no one can outperform them. The worst aspect of this factor is that they expect you to feel them as strongly as they do. They do not want to feel challenged or undervalued, so they can only go so far with partners who can comply with this, even if only on the surface.

BOTH HOT AND COLD

They are skilled at persuading people to win something they require. They can sweet-talk you in favor by using compliments and other means. Many people feel good when they receive compliments.

People's hearts have been won. However, narcissists can go from being in a good mood to being in a bad mood, making you feel discouraged and guilty, and blaming you for things you didn't do.

ABUSE BY NARCISSISTS

This is the abuse associated with a narcissist's relationships. It is a form of emotional abuse perpetrated by narcissists on those close to them. Aside from psychological and emotional abuse, there are also financial, spiritual, sexual, and physical forms of abuse. The relationships listed below are examples of the aforementioned narcissistic abuse.

Workplace research shows that abusers frequently get an easy way up the ranks at work, winning the trust of their co-workers.

Their perceptions give them an advantage in achieving such goals because most of them are considered smart and thus more deserving than their co-workers. Narcissists seek dominance over others and will pursue this goal regardless of the path they take. They are psychopaths who can pit co-workers against each other to gain favor from all sides to advance in the company. This trait has been observed to be more prevalent among managers than among lower-ranking employees.

They use intimidation and harassment to push others down after achieving their "deserved positions" in the company through co-workers. Undermining others is another tactic they use to put down the rest of the workers, giving the impression that they are superior. According to the Workplace Bullying Institute, these are the sources of domestic violence at work where an individual with narcissistic traits is the sole beneficiary. Their actions are morally repugnant, but they often appear unconcerned because their goal is to gain power.

Parent-Child Family Relationships, which keep people together as parent-child or among siblings, create the ideal environment for narcissistic abuse. For example, a narcissistic parent will demand power to control and self-validation, which will be imposed on their children. Misbehavior by a child is regarded as outrageous disobedience.

direct orders from the parent feel completely ignored at the slightest provocation, developing hard feelings that are associated with negative things like corporal punishments.

RELATIONSHIPS IN LOVE

Narcissism develops from a person's self-esteem and sense of entitlement. When a narcissistic partner feels less admirable to their partners, they will demean their partner's appearance. They make fun of their lovers' appearances to feel better or superior to them. Their natural end goal is to boost their ego over their partners, and this is how they make themselves fit their standards.

Their obnoxious tactics extend to publicly humiliating their partners. They enjoy eliciting emotional reactions from their victims by making them feel guilty and humiliated. They can act like sadists, in this case, using gaslighting to make their victims feel guilty and annoyed even before the gatherings. This is their method of seizing and securing control and power over the rest of the people involved as their partners.

A narcissistic love partner will demand to be highly valued, to have his or her grievances addressed quickly, and to be well attended to. A narcissistic relationship also results in frequent threats to the partner. The narcissistic partner will frequently want to make the other partner feel guilty and discouraged, even for the wrongs they have caused. They are associated with shifting blame to their partners; they dig up dirt on a partner to make them look bad.

In a narcissistic relationship, fear and anxiety will always be a part of a partner. The behavior of a narcissistic partner is unpredictable; good times are only a temporary high; they make one feel wanted and valued, but then they can bring regrets the next minute. They are frequently regarded as bright and classic individuals based on how they present themselves socially, physically, and intellectually.

They are, ironically, people who are incapable of forming and maintaining strong social bonds, even with their lovers.

As discussed earlier in this article, narcissistic people tend to disrespect their partners by putting their needs ahead of those of others; in love relationships, they will make a partner feel intimidated. They will be perceived as uncaring and toxic partners in a relationship. This is why anyone in a relationship with a narcissistic person is often advised to end the relationship as soon as possible.

Healthy relationships and narcissism

The characteristics of a good relationship can differ from one couple to the next. In this article, it is appropriate to draw a comparison between a conflicted relationship and a healthy relationship. The following paragraph discusses some characteristics of a healthy or, more accurately, a good relationship.

RESPECT FOR ONE ANOTHER

To build a good relationship, people in a relationship must be positive. The core of this factor is treating each other well, despite any frustrations that someone may be experiencing.

If you must disagree, do so peacefully to make room for a better relationship tomorrow. This is done to avoid the distress that comes with narcissistic relationships.

COMMUNICATION

Those in love should always try to communicate to build trust, which is essential for a peaceful relationship.

Telling your partner where you are, what you are doing, and how your day went is a simple thing to do, but it can protect a relationship.

HAVING FUN BOTH TOGETHER AND APART

Partners require space for friends in addition to lovers and alone time. This allows partners to do what they believe is best for their lives. It should not be viewed as a threat to a relationship because the partners will most likely spend time together separately. That is how to properly introduce a person to others who could be supportive friends. Nobody should feel trapped in a healthy relationship; too much shielding can also lead to unintended consequences.

SINCERITY AND FIDELITY

In a relationship, honesty leads to fidelity, which is the foundation of trust. Trust determines how long a relationship will last and how healthy it will become over time. In the absence of these characteristics, there will be no true love between the couples if they have a relationship.

Untrustworthiness is the source of silent enmity and cheating, resulting in bitter disagreements and regrettable breakups in narcissistic relationships.

A FULFILLING SEXUAL LIFE

In a good relationship, pushing a partner beyond their comfortable sex levels is unnecessary. It is desirable to break the intervals of having it done, but the most rewarding sex life is what is important here. Trying new things that will better suit your partner could also be a useful contribution to optimizing your sex life.

EMPATHY

Feeling for each other is an obvious sign of a good couple's friendship. They should make each other feel wanted in both good and bad times. In a healthy relationship, sounding positive, supportive, and appreciating each other's ideas, as well as attempting to see things from your partner's perspective, is likable. People in a marriage must value each other equally, or the other partner will feel unappreciated.

NARCISSISM IN THE SHADOWS

Also known as "closet narcissism." Victims of this condition do not display entitlement and self-made superiority in the same way that true narcissists do. They have low self-esteem and are curious about how others perceive them. They silently seek to understand how others perceive them, even those close to them.

Covert narcissists are also described as silent and sensitive individuals who must be treated with caution. They are difficult to recognize due to their silence and silent nature; identifying them requires an internalized experience.

They are similar to narcissists in that they use those they perceive to be inferior to themselves to gain superiority. In their preferred environment, they appear to exhibit manipulative and entitlement traits similar to narcissists. They regard themselves as superior beings and seek attention to place themselves in front of their colleagues wherever they are. Normally, this is their plan to get what they want and get into positions of power.

HOW TO SPOT SUBTLE NARCISSISM IN A RELATIONSHIP

People suffering from narcissism are often socially upright and do not bother their families. However, in the case of untreated narcissistic personality disorder (NPD), an individual will exhibit traits such as manipulation and neglect. The signs of a covert narcissistic relationship are as follows.

INSENSITIVITY TO THE PARTNER

Such people in a relationship can be identified by a lack of affection and support. They are heartless as if they are unaffected by what their partner is going through.

A SENSE OF INFERIORITY

The person suffering from NPD will feel less valued and insecure in their relationships. In some cases, it appears normal, but when combined with other factors, it is a proven sign of covert narcissism.

A PARTNER'S CONTEMPT

Contempt in a relationship can be hidden in silence, but it is still lethal for the damage it can cause. A partner or family member may dislike another partner or family member quietly, only to express it through dismissiveness and mild negativity.

STRENUOUS EFFORTS TO GAIN YOUR SYMPATHY

A covert narcissist has an uncanny ability to elicit sympathy from their partners. They can impersonate a condition to get your attention. They frequently want you to attend to them, as do people who lack confidence in themselves. They are attention seekers who will go as far as to fake illness.

Another sign of covert narcissism among victims is the proclivity to step in and help to gain recognition.

THE RECOVERY FROM A NARCISSISTIC RELATIONSHIP

Individuals who have been in stressful or traumatizing relationships are usually emotionally scarred. They require assistance in resuming normalcy. Therapists take this seriously because someone may have lost confidence in themselves, causing their self-esteem to plummet.

These effects are the result of their intimidation and frustration. Healing from narcissistic relationships is a step that must be guided psychologically. They are listed below.

REFUTING YOUR FALSE BELIEFS

Make a list of the beliefs you have about your former partner that are preventing you from moving on. Such a list may include statements such as "you'll never find someone else like your ex-lover," "you should have done something to make the relationship work," "he could have treated the next lover better than me," and other negatives that may prevent you from letting go. This is usually reserved for those who believe they are to blame more than their ex-lovers.

YOU MUST LEARN WHO ENCOURAGED YOU TO ACCEPT FULL RESPONSIBILITY.

This has the effect of allowing you to recognize that it could simply be a habit of taking responsibility for themselves and not that they are always at fault. It can assist someone in relearning to forgive themselves and live as free individuals, free of any form of guilt. They can then judge and review life situations, and they may realize that they were not the only ones who caused breakups.

Consider what you stand to gain by protecting your ex and blaming yourself.

This stage allows you to reflect on what happened in your relationship, consider the benefits of staying with your ex, and consider what you miss about your ex.

CREATE STATEMENTS THAT ADDRESS THE BELIEFS THAT KEEP YOU BOUND TO YOUR EX.

These are the statements that will help you get off the hook and free yourself from guilt. Such statements could include, he is likely to abuse the new lover as well, and the breakup was not entirely my fault. Statements should be made from the heart, breaking down what is harmful to your psychological health.

Chapter 5

HANDLING THE NARCISSIST,

Narcissism is extremely harmful to victims, and unless they know how to best deal with a narcissist, they may suffer the consequences for the rest of their lives. Identifying the type of narcissist, one is dealing with is a major step toward understanding how bad the situation is. At times, one may wish to assist the narcissist, but this is almost always impossible. The best way is for you to change how you see and treat them, as well as how much attention you give them.

Narcissists, in most cases, do not change. They will only pretend to trap you, and if you fall for it, they will revert to their old ways. They are always hoping for a victim to fall for it because they know how vulnerable you can be. They will then use this against you. Consider the following when dealing with such scenarios:

DETERMINE THE TYPE OF NARCISSIST WITH WHOM YOU ARE DEALING.

Once you've determined that the traits, you're observing in someone are narcissistic, try to figure out which type they are.

Because not all are created equal, how you handle one should be primarily determined by the type you are dealing with. According to research, there are two types of narcissists:

Vulnerable narcissist: This personality type has an outward sense of self-importance that conceals a weak inner self. These narcissists are usually emotionally unstable and use manipulation to compensate for their low self-esteem. They are also sadder and put on a lot of masks to hide their failures.

Such people may have been broken by a bad experience, and they will then project their negativity onto others. They, too, enjoy being recognized and will go to great lengths to achieve it.

It takes a long time for people to notice them. This is only to satisfy their ego, which never lasts long because they are fighting internal battles. Such situations necessitate a thorough understanding of where they are coming from and their need for validation.

Narcissists with lofty ambitions: These people believe and think too highly of themselves, and they are not always as good as they believe. These are the worst, and they have mastered the art of belittling everyone and demonstrating their superiority while ignoring everyone's feelings or opinions.

They are the know-it-all who is generally happier and more naturally extroverted. Such narcissists can be great assets in some situations because they are obsessed with getting things done just to be recognized and appreciated. They will also always want to prove themselves, so they will work the hardest.

It is much easier to deal with them once you know which type you are dealing with. This is because once you know what irritates them or makes them feel good about themselves, you can easily work on avoiding certain situations or knowing how to best handle them.

CONSIDER THEM FOR WHAT THEY ARE.

Narcissists are very manipulative by nature, which can make them very popular because they know how to act. They are mostly charming, which attracts those who do not know them well and leads them to believe they are wonderful people. Unfortunately, this never lasts because their true colors are always revealed.

Once you've known them for who they are, it's important to keep your distance, understand the type of people they are, and not place too many expectations on them. There is no reason to give a narcissist so many more chances once you have established their true character. You only end up hurting yourself because narcissists rarely change.

A predator will always be a predator. And it is what gives them their energy. When they realize they have power, they become manipulative.

Some people manipulate to fulfill their evil desires. This is what one must understand to avoid falling victim to their enticement and deception.

Stand up to them and advocate for yourself.

There are times when you should keep quiet and keep your distance from a narcissist, but there are also times when you should stand up to them and speak for yourself. This is largely determined by your relationship with the person in question, as well as how close you are to each other. A parent or spouse is an example. You have to deal with and live with these people for the majority of your life, so ignoring them is not an option.

This option is best for people you care about and want to keep close or the relationship going. You must inform them that their words and actions are hurting you and that you would appreciate it if they changed or stopped completely.

Be consistent with it whenever it occurs so that they are aware that their behavior is inappropriate. Even if you do this, be prepared for it to fail or for the narcissist to take some time to change.

SET FIRM LIMITS ON PERSONAL ITEMS.

The majority of narcissists lack boundaries and have no sense of personal space. They tend to pick things or enter other people's spaces without considering how it affects the person. They may appear to ignore such important aspects at times, but they simply do not see the boundaries. They need to be reminded frequently that boundaries should be established and followed. Make reminding them a habit so that they are aware and it sticks. When you let them get away with crossing them, they become accustomed to it and see it as no big deal when they do so. If they are in your personal space, make it clear when they are crossing the line. Having clear boundaries makes it easier to avoid falling victim to the abuser's deception. It also creates a safe environment for you.

RECOGNIZE THAT THEY REQUIRE ASSISTANCE.

People who exhibit such characteristics frequently require assistance. They may not realize it, but they may be suffering from a disorder that necessitates professional assistance. Most of the time, they will never seek help because they consider themselves to be normal, just like any other person. Knowing what causes the behavior can help them get the necessary assistance.

If you suggest this when they are at their worst, they may interpret it negatively. Ascertain that they are in a good mood, and suggest that they seek professional assistance while emphasizing that the decision must be made by them.

If they express an interest in receiving assistance, you can intervene and provide additional information about the options available to them. If you believe you have excellent contacts, connect them and let them handle the rest. Change is always a personal choice and effort, so it must originate with them.

DETERMINE THE SOURCE OF THE BEHAVIOR.

It is extremely beneficial to understand where the behavior is coming from and what causes it. This may be determined by the nature of your relationship with the individual. Following similar experiences, some people develop narcissism as a survival strategy. Some people become that way as a means of survival to conceal their inner weak selves. Such people would require a boost in confidence or affirmation.

Once you understand where it all began, you will react differently because it is not always their fault that they behave in this manner. They simply do not know any better. Once you've figured this out, it'll be easier to support them or know what kind of help you can get them.

Other times, you will be able to identify what situations trigger the abuse and avoid them.

TOTAL SEPARATION

However, depending on how close you are to the person, you may need to completely separate yourself from the relationship. This is most common when there is violence involved or when the abuse is so severe that it interferes with one's daily life.

IF YOU HAVE TO DEAL WITH A TOXIC NARCISSISTIC PERSON DAILY,

Keeping a safe distance may be the best option for maintaining peace and sanity.

It is more difficult in the case of a close family relation, such as a mother, sibling, spouse, etc., because this is a family. Most people will say family first because they are the closest relatives one has; however, when it comes to abuse, one must sometimes choose. When it is clear that it is no longer working, take a big step away from the abuse. You have the option of moving out, leaving that abusive spouse, finding a new job, or simply ending some friendships.

This allows you to reset and gain a clear perspective on how you want to handle the situation. It also means that the narcissist will lose power over them.

BE CONSIDERATE.

In such a situation, this is one of the most difficult things to do. Being sympathetic to someone who has offended you. Narcissists, like any other human being, do not necessarily have feelings.

They simply do not understand how to interact with others. Being compassionate does not imply ignoring the fact that they are offensive, but rather admitting that they have a problem and taking on the role of the bigger person. It entails focusing on the positive aspects of their personality rather than their flaws. There are several approaches to this:

Slightly confirm them. Do not overdo it, as this will only make the abuser feel proud and encourage them to continue their bad behavior. This affirmation is intended to let them know that they have a positive side that they can develop. It also gives them hope of becoming better people.

Ignore their criticism: Do not entertain them when they are having a bad day. Get busy so they don't have an audience. Even if it means leaving, do it so they know no one wants to deal with their negative energy. This may be difficult, but it is the best option. A narcissist who lacks an audience or targets will feel powerless. It does, however, require someone tough enough to ignore even negative comments directed at them without taking them personally.

Inform them that they have a problem. You can do this when they are calm and assure them that there is assistance available. This causes them to reflect on why they do certain things and may provide an opportunity to assist them in working on themselves.

Being compassionate only causes narcissists to reconsider their character and realize that they can be better people. It is worthwhile to try, but due to the nature of the person, they are unlikely to notice your efforts. Do it with an open mind, knowing that they may interpret everything negatively rather than seeing the effort you are making to help them.

MANAGING THE AFTEREFFECTS OF ABUSE

After dealing with a narcissist and figuring out how to handle them, there is also the aftermath of the abuse to deal with. This ensures that clear goals have been established to improve and avoid further abuse. It is also beneficial to the individual because it assists them in dealing with any trauma caused by the abuser. If such issues are not addressed, people may become bitter and project their feelings onto others.

These steps are more beneficial to the victim and focus on what they can do for themselves rather than the abuser:

SET FIRM BOUNDARIES.

To begin healing, one must build walls or protect themselves from the abuser. Set clear boundaries for yourself once you've figured out how to deal with the abuser. Remember your decisions to leave an abusive relationship and use them to set boundaries. If a request is denied, let it be denied, no matter how much the abuser claims to have changed.

NARCISSISTS SELDOM CHANGE.

This is the first step toward healing and dealing with abuse. Keep your distance and don't look back if you're keeping it.

Avoid them as much as possible because any interaction will trigger memories or trigger another round of abuse. If this does not work, you can do it psychologically by removing them from your thoughts. This can be difficult, especially if you are constantly interacting with the narcissist or are in the same environment. However, it ends up boosting your confidence and self-esteem because they will no longer be able to bring you down.

RECOGNIZE WHEN YOU REQUIRE ASSISTANCE AND SEEK IT.

Prolonged abuse is extremely harmful to an individual and may result in future adult problems. Examine yourself more deeply and recognize when you require professional assistance. Given your situation, it may be difficult.

Although you are not the source of the problem, it is always better to be safe than sorry. The effects of abuse typically take time to manifest, and they may not manifest until you are well into adulthood. This is why it is critical to seek assistance and speak with someone about the events. This aids in the healing and release of any accumulated rage and bitterness.

Someone who was abused by their mother as a child is an example. They grow into successful men or women, get married, have children, and then the past comes back to haunt them. They begin abusing their children. And because they never sought closure or assistance and didn't know any better, the cycle unfortunately continues. Because they don't know any better, it's becoming increasingly difficult for them to change their ways of thinking or acting. This is a strong indication that the victim requires assistance as well.

It helps them avoid subjecting other people to the same abuse they have experienced, believing it is the norm.

LOCATE A SUPPORT SYSTEM.

Create a new healthy relationship or strengthen an existing one. This should begin to function as your support system, people you can confidently turn to when you are feeling down or in need of encouragement. Man is not an island, and this would be extremely beneficial in such circumstances. Spending too much time alone will only cause you to think more about certain issues and may make you sad about what has already happened to you.

When you have a support system, you can spend more time doing positive things and interacting with them, which keeps you busy and helps you see life in a positive light. As the saying goes, the devil's workshop is an idle mind. Make an effort to avoid being idle and lonely. This is risky because one may find themselves returning to old abusive relationships just for the company.

Participate in fun activities and spend more time building relationships with the new support system. Replace the old, ineffective ones with new ones.

ones that are nutritious A typical healthy relationship: Is not judgmental: Your friends should not judge you based on your bad experiences. Instead, they shape you into a better person. Seek out friendships that see the best in you and work to cultivate it.

It boosts your self-esteem: Positive friendships boost one's self-esteem. They will make someone feel good about themselves rather than focusing on what they are not. Look for it in your friendships. A friend should not make you feel inferior or unwelcome. They inspire you to be the best you can be.

Respectful of your opinions and decisions: If there is any negativity in a situation or friendship, the decision to leave is entirely yours, and good friends will understand when you are unable to participate in certain activities.

● Maintain healthy boundaries: Develop boundaries-respecting friendships. When your no is taken as a no, there is an issue. Maintain friends who will understand if you need to be away from them. Or when you need to recharge your batteries.

Is concerned about your well-being and mental health: Because there is always a lot of trauma that comes with abuse, you need a circle that understands this and will support you in getting over it, rather than constantly reminding you of what could have been.

If a relationship does not make you feel appreciated and as if you belong, it is not worth cultivating.

RECOGNIZE THAT YOU ARE NOT TO BLAME.

Victims of abuse frequently blame themselves for the abuse, believing that they are to blame for what has occurred. Narcissists are notorious for projecting their negativity onto their victims, making them feel guilty for things they did not do.

It is critical that you understand this right away because it is a path to healing.

It is never your fault if someone treats you poorly. It primarily reflects who they are rather than who you are. You must remember this so that you are not held responsible for their bad behavior or bad experiences. Taking the blame prevents you from standing up for yourself or knowing when to remove yourself from a situation. Instead, it will make you feel as if you owe your allegiance to the abuser. Improve your self-esteem and confidence, and keep in mind that negativity directed at you is not your fault and should not be tolerated.

WHY DID THE NARCISSIST PICK YOU?

It can be difficult to walk away from a relationship with a Narcissist, especially one that you have nurtured for a long time. Many people believe that fighting for their relationship and their partner is healthy, but there are times when you should walk away.

When it comes to a person who abuses you, it can be difficult to know what to do. Narcissists, as we've seen in previous chapters, aren't the best people to be in a relationship with. They have this strange habit of coming up with story after story just to keep you interested while playing with your self-esteem.

But what made you the ideal prey for the narcissist? Remember that the person did not choose you at random and that he took his time to bring you into his orbit. Narcissist knows what they want in a partner, and you might be the perfect match for them.

Usually, the victims appear to have gotten involved with the person rather than the other way around. One minute you're harmlessly flirting with this guy, and the next you're so deeply in love with him that you can't remember what happened to get you to this point.

This is because narcissists have been bred to be masters of survival. They can identify and listen to people who will fall into their loop. They know the person will stick around and look after their needs, even if they have revealed their inner destructive habits.

- So, who is the ideal prey for a narcissist?
- You have what they desire.

A narcissist is on the lookout for a "narcissistic supply." The individual is looking for that one thing that will feed his ego, keep him pumped up, and protect him from the fragile view that he has of himself.

They want admiration, fame, money, compliments, and good looks, as well as an image of a perfect family and a prestigious career.

If you have a problem with how they act for whatever reason, they will not be interested in you.

SEXUALLY

When you decide to date a narcissist, they may be looking for physical stimulation and for you to compliment their performance after a sexual encounter, even if they don't deserve it.

They want to be with you because they know you will compliment them when they do something nice for you. They don't care how or what you feel during the act; all they want is for you to compliment their ability.

If they discover that you can be sexually controlled, they will crave you even more because they know they have control over you.

What Qualities Does a Narcissist Seek in a Woman?

You will be swept off your feet with fancy dinners, compliments, and gifts you never expected to receive – you will believe you have found Mr. Right when in reality you are a pawn in a chess game.

The romance will be out of this world, and you will feel as if you are in a movie, but this will only last long enough for you to realize that everything in the relationship revolves around him, and you are always on the periphery.

He constantly talks about what he is about and what he does, and in all situations prioritizes his needs over yours. He is sensitive to criticism and is always obsessed with what he does because it all comes down to status. You'll realize that the expensive dinner dates at high-end restaurants were just part of the game.

Let's take a look at the top qualities that a narcissist seeks in a woman.

YOU ARE SUCCESSFUL, BUT YOU ARE INSECURE.

You may not admit it, but if you are insecure and continue to admit it, even if you are attractive, you may be advertising yourself to be suitable for the narcissist.

The narcissist seeks someone who fits the description of someone who will make them look good. And if you have good looks and a good job but always feel like you don't belong, they will easily make you feel like a hero.

They are drawn to you not because you are beautiful and accomplished; rather, they want your appearance and achievements to boost their ego.

However, they do not want to be with a woman who is overconfident because she may be in control, which they do not want. Instead, they want to be in charge of the show all of the time.

If he senses your insecurity, he will be more drawn to you because you will not stand in the way of his success, whether fake or real. If the narcissist detects your level of self-assurance, he will turn and walk away.

So, how does someone who is the insecure act? If you have any of the following characteristics, you should be aware that you are insecure:

You put yourself down. How much you value yourself is determined by your self-worth. If you always accept less, you will feel worthy and will never believe that you deserve more. You will accept less than a normal person would.

They make fun of others. Insecure people tend to put others down to feel better about themselves as a result of their insecurities. They have been putting themselves down for so long that they believe they must also treat others in this manner. They want to bring others down so that they can rise to their level.

You imitate others. Insecure people lack the confidence to create something on their own. They believe that if they come up with something on their own, it will be insufficient to work for them, or they will be judged for their poor show. As a result, they stick to their comfort zone and then imitate those who are more successful.

YOU ARE A PEOPLE PLEASER.

We all want the person we date to be happy, but if it comes at the expense of your happiness and well-being, it has become unhealthy.

The narcissist is looking for the person who will give him the attention he craves and the emotional validation he craves. If you don't have a strong sense of what you want, the narcissist will quickly take over.

The narcissist seeks to monopolize the relationship and will never compromise on his desires. He is always demanding what he requires. If he realizes you have boundaries that you adhere to, he will flee so quickly that you will be surprised.

SIGNS THAT YOU ARE A PEOPLE PLEASER INCLUDE:

You act as if you agree with everyone. When you are a people pleaser, you will listen to other people's opinions even if you disagree with them. You're pretending to agree with them just to make them like you, even if what they represent disagrees with you.

You hold people accountable for their actions. It is always beneficial to understand how your actions affect others, but believing that you have complete control over their happiness becomes a major issue. It is up to you to maintain control over your emotions. Don't always hold people accountable for their actions because it encourages them to take advantage of you.

You are constantly sorry. If you find yourself constantly blaming yourself for things you haven't done, or if you suspect that others are constantly blaming you for things you haven't done, you should be cautious. Frequent apologies are always a sign of weakness and a larger problem. Don't be afraid to be yourself.

You are always doing things for others. If you are a pleaser, your schedule will always be full of activities that you do for other people, even if they aren't necessary.

You never refuse. Do you realize you have the authority to say no to things that don't make sense to you?

The unfortunate reality is that many people do not know when to say no.

They will eventually accept anything that comes their way and will say yes to things they know they are incapable of doing.

When someone is angry at them, they feel bad. Just because someone is upset doesn't mean you're wrong. If you can't bear the thought of someone being angry at you, you're more likely to abandon your values.

You imitate those around you. If you find yourself doing things just to make the other person happy, you will end up attracting a narcissist.

You value compliments. While a little praise and kind words can make anyone feel good, pleasers are looking for a lot of validation for everything they do. If you believe that your worth is solely determined by what other people think of you, you will only feel good when you are complimented on anything you do.

At all costs, you avoid conflict. It's one thing not to want to start a fight, but if you're always avoiding fights at all costs, it means you're working hard to stand up for what you believe in.

When you are hurt, you do not admit it. If you have been hurt many times and are unwilling to tell the person who has hurt you your feelings, you are the ideal target for a narcissist. If you can't stand up and express your sadness, embarrassment, and anger after someone has done something to you, the narcissist will exploit this to further harm you.

AT ALL COSTS, YOU AVOID CONFLICT.

Some people enjoy conflict. If, on the other hand, you tend to avoid all conflict, you will become more appealing to the narcissist. Narcissist seeks someone who will cooperate with them even when they are at odds. You are the ideal partner for the narcissist if you easily give in to their demands or wishes, whether at work or in your personal life.

If you are constantly putting your needs aside to make things work in the face of conflict, you will fall prey to the narcissist, who thrives when you give them the attention and empathy that they crave. Being compromised in a relationship is beneficial, but when you are a doormat, you only receive negative consequences.

To avoid situations, you change the subject. You can make a joke, be passive-aggressive, leave the room, or purposefully change the subject to avoid continuing the confrontation. You will come up if you are avoiding a conflict with something that will get you out of it or make it more peaceful

You work as a gunnysack. Here, you silently accumulate annoyances and grievances, then let them build up before releasing them in a burst. This is a sign that you haven't resolved issues as you go, and instead, you hold on to them.

You suffer in silence. You should understand that as an adult, you will resolve some issues through conflict. If you tend to suffer in silence, the conflicts will accumulate and may end up causing your depression.

You are afraid of expressing yourself. If you are in a relationship, you should understand that your fights are all about expressing your position in ways that will persuade the other person that they are wrong. However, if you have difficulty telling the other person your side of the story or standing up for a particular point, you are a pushover.

YOU IGNORE WARNING SIGNS

One of the most obvious red flags that a person is a narcissist is that they never accept responsibility for the negative events in their lives. They are notorious for playing the victim even when they are the ones who are at fault. They will always blame their bosses, ex-partners, and friends for what has happened to them in the past.

Make the mistake of ignoring any indications that the person is a narcissist. They will tell you that they left their previous job because the boss was after them, or that their previous relationship failed because their ex was a stalker, and so on.

We all make mistakes, but if someone does not accept responsibility for their actions at all times, you will jeopardize your progress and happiness because the next person he will blame will be you.

YOU FALL IN LOVE SO QUICKLY.

It's not a bad thing to fall in love with someone, but if you do it too quickly, you'll be the perfect recipe for the narcissist. When you are in love, the narcissist will take advantage of this and make it work for him.

Let us examine the indicators that indicate to the narcissist that you are prey, and that you will be easy for him to exploit for his pleasure.

You are blind to the flaws. The narcissist will come to you with many flaws, but when you are deeply in love with someone, you will not notice the flaws and will believe the person is perfect. You'll fall in love with what you see and forget what you feel.

You have self-centered desires. When you are madly in love with someone, you will go to great lengths to ensure that they are always with you.

You will frequently forget your tasks and responsibilities just to be with the person. The narcissist will notice this quickly and take advantage of it.

You begin to feel possessive. You will crave the person's constant presence. You will most likely demand that they spend all of their time with you, which will make you possessive and insecure.

You come to a halt. If you have been proving to yourself that you are rational, you will have illogical thoughts when you become infatuated. You'll be perplexed as to why your brain has become attached to the object of your "love." What you must understand is that the narcissist will notice this and exploit it in ways you are unaware of.

You lose concentration. The narcissist wants you to call them all the time, telling them how much you love them and how you can't live without them. You will notice that your mind wanders back to your memories of the narcissist. You don't seem to be performing at your best because you've lost focus and shifted it to the person.

Chapter 6

WOMEN'S FANTASIES MAKE THEM EASY PREY FOR THE NARCISSIST

If you've ever been in love with a narcissist, you know he'll always tell you who he is and what he does. He will keep telling you this until you fall for his trap and realize it is all your fault.

These goals will be revealed through his actions and the way he treats you.

Yes, you will have doubts, but you will ignore them because you are blinded by the "love" he gives you.

Instead of learning from your mistakes and exiting the train, there are a few fantasies that will entice you to see exactly what you want to see and to believe in the promises, words, and illusions that he creates.

As a result, he will leave you spinning tale after tale about how he is the best person, looking for reasons to stay with him, and then wondering why nothing you do makes him happy - or why, despite what you do for him, he remains sad.

- It's all because of the fantasies you've created in your mind.
- You must demonstrate your ability to support your man.

You want to show the world that you are a good woman who will support her man. According to society, a good woman values male dominance, privilege, and supremacy. You will find appreciation and value if you sacrifice your well-being, which means accepting the treatment you receive from the man.

This is one of the rules that govern cults, where male dominance is attributed to God.

The truth is that this fantasy is just a ploy to draw you deeper into the person's trap. You will begin to participate in your abuse, and you will be enticed to believe that you will feel good while suffering.

WHAT A NARCISSIST DESIRES IN BED

Without getting intimate, a relationship is incomplete. When you become intimate with the narcissist, you will notice a few signs that will make you doubt your abilities.

Consider what the narcissist expects from you when you get intimate.

1. EXCELLENCE

He will want you to be perfect in bed, even if he isn't.

When you sleep with them, one of the sensations you will have is that you are walking on eggshells. You will feel like a student summoned by the principal for making an error.

You have the feeling that you will be called at any moment because you may not have met their expectations at all, or you may have disappointed them in some way. They will use aggression when you do not meet their standards, and may even physically abuse you to demonstrate their dominance.

Because narcissist has an inflated sense of self, they frequently regard the people with whom they are intimate as objects that are supposed to meet their needs. When they are disappointed, they will frequently blame, criticize, and confront you to make you feel like the victim.

Because you never know when the next outburst will occur, the relationship will always be tense.

2. HE IS IN COMMAND.

Another common characteristic is the narcissist's obsession with controlling everything that occurs in the bedroom. They will want you to respond exactly to what they want, and they will know what will happen when you get intimate. If things don't go their way, they will become enraged and may even blame you for what happened. The prospect of losing control over what they have in sight is often terrifying to the narcissist, and they will go to great lengths to ensure that it does not occur.

This can be as simple as being late for that intimate date or not doing things the way he expects.

3. HE BECOMES ENRAGED SO QUICKLY

One of the narcissist's common characteristics is that he will erupt into a rage if you ask him why things aren't going well. You'll be intimate one moment, then he'll be so enraged the next that you'll wonder what's wrong.

When this happens, you will be shell-shocked and shaken, unsure of what is going on.

4. AVERSION BUT OBSESSION

The narcissist's attitude toward sex is one of avoidance while also becoming obsessive. They don't want to show how much they need you to please them, even though they do.

This action stems from their feelings of shame and guilt, which drive their thoughts.

The narcissist will make you feel horrible about yourself after the session. You will feel betrayed, used, and disgusted, and you may even begin to doubt your sexual identity. You will be made to believe all sorts of things about yourself that are completely false.

This is concerning because, if you recall, things were going well at first. You had the most fun and connected on a deeper level.

5. SURPRISING GENEROSITY

You'll be surprised at how generous the narcissist can be in bed.

You may perceive them to be hit-and-run types, but you will be surprised to discover that they are expert lovers who will aim to provide you with orgasm after orgasm while also providing you with the best experience ever.

The only disadvantage is that they may expect you to give something in return or explain the details after the sex.

THEY ARE PARTICULAR

Narcissist has particular sexual preferences that they pursue. They may have specific and explicit ideas about what you should do in bed.

what you should do or say They want the intimacy to unfold in a certain way, which can result in strained experiences and even boredom on your part.

They are typically less experimental than others. They are always looking for ways to portray themselves as in command or manipulative. They will boast about how good they are in bed, only to reveal that they are limited to only two positions. They will avoid doing anything that will make them appear foolish, and they will go to great lengths to please you.

They are constantly self-conscious about their appearance. As a result, they can stifle any creativity in the bedroom and will take pictures before and after sex. They will also film themselves in the act. If you sleep with one, you will undoubtedly appear in one of the mages or on the video.

7. UNABLE TO HANDLE CRITICISM

A narcissist will never learn from his mistakes, and he will rarely admit to making any mistakes. The narcissist will not ask you what you like in bed, but will make certain that he does what he enjoys the most; it is up to you to love or hate him for this.

If you try to give them feedback on their performance after they have been praised for it, they will claim you are wrong and will degrade your sexual desires to make you feel bad. They'll try to convince you that they're not interested in you when their bodies are screaming otherwise.

The first time you tell them they aren't perfect in bed; they will react with rage and ridicule. They will tell you how incorrect you are and how you did not arouse them in the least. You will be made to feel insane because they believe they know what they are talking about. 8. It's Always About Them

Even if the intimacy is perfect, you will always notice that it is all about them and not about you. The experience will be unique because, in other relationships, you talk and connect with the other person.

Another person, you must listen to him blow his trumpet about what he just did.

Chapter 7

NARCISSISM IN SOCIETY,

These days, many people are labeled as narcissists, including presidential candidates, co-workers, movie stars, and even millennials. This word appears to be used far more frequently than it was previously.

The truth is that we have narcissists in society today, and with their presence come to a slew of issues, particularly the need to understand them and work closely with them as members of society.

Let us examine the prevalence of this disorder in society and what you can do to address it.

WORKING PLACE NARCISSISM

The narcissist at your workplace can be extremely annoying and frustrating. They may even pose a serious threat to your professional prospects. The question is, how will you know if the person with whom you are working is a narcissist?

THEY DOMINATE THE CONVERSATION AND CONSTANTLY INTERRUPT YOU.

They will interrupt the conversation and then sway everyone to their side to begin talking about themselves. Many narcissists are self-centered and will go on and on about their accomplishments, projects, and personal life.

They have an uncanny ability to find something to talk about even when it isn't particularly important to anyone else in the office.

When you talk about something unrelated to them, they will show little or no interest and will quickly shift the focus to themselves. They will talk a lot about themselves because they enjoy hearing themselves speak.

2. WILL REMIND YOU OF THEIR VALUE

Aside from dominating conversations in such a way that you feel belittled, some narcissists will constantly remind you of who they are and what role they play in the company. They will remind you of how much they earn, which is more than yours, and they will also want to tell you about their degrees and how important they are to the company.

They will discuss the people they meet and the high-profile projects they are working on in comparison to what you have.

That is not a good thing to do. They will discuss the prestigious schools they have attended and their grades.

They want to stay important in the organization, so they will blow up an exaggerated version of themselves to make you fear them.

3. ATTENTION SEEKER

They enjoy being the center of attention and will attempt to achieve this by dominating meetings, conferences, presentations, and email.

discussions. When they participate in discussions, they constantly remind the attendees of their accomplishments and will feel bad if someone less qualified speaks before them.

They will try to argue that their contributions require special consideration at all times.

Some narcissists will take advantage of the opportunity to disrupt the meeting and put people down. All they want is to be as powerful and influential as possible.

4. THEY CLAIM CREDIT THAT WAS NOT INTENDED FOR THEM

Some narcissists will try to implement ideas proposed by their colleagues. They will attempt to take credit for something they did not do, or they will attempt to steal the recognition directly.

You will hear complaints from their co-workers about items they have stolen from them. These people will show you what they did and how they did it, but the narcissist will give you a different version.

Many times, they do not even handle a significant portion of the project, but they will take the lead once the project is completed. They don't work as hard as everyone else, and they don't contribute much - all they do is have their name added to the list of those who have contributed.

5. ENTHUSIASTIC, BUT NEVER DELIVERS

Many narcissists are charismatic and will sell whatever the company has for sale. But they have one problem: they refuse to follow up on what they sell because they believe they don't have the time.

They can persuade a client to purchase because they typically create favorable impressions and will make people believe in what they do or say, as well as manipulate people to get what they want.

In a real sense, these narcissists are lacking in substance.

Under the grandiose ideas are broken promises and unfulfilled expectations have not been met, and deadlines have been missed

Many of them will claim to have learned their lessons and will do so to manipulate you into supporting their next scheme.

6. DISOBEY A SLEW OF RULES

Many narcissists believe they are entitled to preferential treatment and thus are above reproach. They will take shortcuts and take advantage of the system and other people.

They will falsify reports to suit their needs and steal office supplies to get started. They will make up excuses to miss work and then show up later looking refreshed.

Many narcissists believe they are above the law and should be exempt from its provisions.

7. CONSTANTLY BLAMING OTHERS FOR THEIR FAILURES

These narcissists are always averse to criticism; they don't take any negative feedback when sitting down and will try to shoot it down if you make them appear malleable.

They don't want anything to jeopardize their image or status and will react angrily to any accusation leveled against them.

They will always find a way to blame you. They have no qualms about making sure you get fired because of something they did - as long as they save their skin, they don't mind letting you take the fall.

8. WILL NOT TREAT PEOPLE AS EQUALS

Many narcissists are unable to relate to other people as equals. They will either take a position that is inferior to others and then defer to you, or they will assume that they are superior to you in some way.

They lack the empathy to treat people as equal beings; they always see them as distinct from others.

9. FEEL NEGATIVE EMOTIONS

The narcissist will enjoy spreading and eliciting negative emotions to feel powerful, gain attention, and throw you off guard.

They are easily irritated when things do not go their way. They will become enraged if you disagree with them or fail to meet their expectations.

10. THEY LOVE YOU ONE MINUTE AND DESPISE YOU THE NEXT.

A narcissist sees everything in black and white. They will only love you if you do what is right for them, but they will hate you if you change. So, when you notice that they are kind, go ahead and enjoy it, but keep in mind that they are only preparing you for the next session of taking you down.

When you realize they are buttering you up, you must be cautious and avoid them.

11. THEY RARELY APOLOGIZE

The narcissist will refuse to apologize for causing a shambles. They will always try to find a way to blame the mistake on you.

MANAGING A NARCISSIST AT WORK

Just because you work with a narcissist doesn't mean you have to deal with their problems. Remember that if you leave everything as it is, you will be stressed the entire day. Let's take a look at how you handle a narcissist at work.

1. IGNORE THEIR BEHAVIOUR

Ignoring a worker who brags about their abilities is the best way to deal with them. You will be setting yourself up for a power struggle that may never end if you try to engage them. Instead, try to concentrate on your work and then keep your distance to survive.

2. PAY ATTENTION WHEN THEY BEGIN GASLIGHTING

A colleague or boss who engages in gaslighting will show signs of it early on. You must exercise caution to recognize the signs that the boss is acting inappropriately.

The boss may question a specific incident's memory, deny abusive behavior, or change the subject. All of this is designed to make you doubt yourself, and the actions they take will make you believe there is something wrong with you.

When you notice this, you should always walk away to avoid becoming a pawn in the game.

3. DO NOT DEFY THEM

If you are conversing with the narcissist in public, resist the urge to challenge them. This is especially true if they believe you have intentionally harmed their self-image.

When you argue with them, they usually take it personally, and you will be disappointed with the outcome.

4. COMPREHEND THEM

We all know that narcissists have a sense of insecurity that they cling to keep you feeding it. When you understand that they have a disorder, you will understand why they behave the way they do, and you will be able to empathize with them.

5. RECOGNIZE THAT THEY WILL NOT CHANGE.

If you have been with a narcissist for a long time, you will notice that the change they profess never manifests in the way you desire. All they have to do is adjust and adapt to the situation at hand.

You will understand why they do certain things once you understand that they cannot change, and you will not be disappointed when they do something that does not appeal to you.

So, expect the narcissist to continue behaving badly and prepare for it as best you can. Try to figure out what to say to them, stand your ground in meetings, and then organize with others so he doesn't push you over.

6. ESTABLISH BOUNDARIES

When dealing with a narcissist, you must establish and maintain boundaries. These boundaries are critical because they define the boundaries to which people can travel

Learn to say no when your boundaries are crossed and to defend yourself when a narcissist attacks you. Know what to say and when to say it to avoid falling victim to the narcissist's whims.

7. SEEK ASSISTANCE

You should sit down with your boss or a friend and devise a strategy for dealing with such people who bother you at work.

Don't be afraid to seek the advice of others who have witnessed what you are going through.

8. MAKE THEM LOOK BETTER

This may appear to be a little manipulative, but when you praise someone, you gain access to the narcissist's performance at work. If you must delegate a task to them, try to convince them that they are the best people for the job and that you are confident they will deliver flawless results.

Offer the person your attention before, during, and after the job to ensure that things go as planned.

WHAT ARE THE CHARACTERISTICS OF NARCISSISTIC LEADERS?

Aside from workers, we have leaders with narcissistic tendencies. They are only concerned with themselves and will prioritize certain interests. They are arrogant, dominant, and hostile.

When they are driven by the desire for admiration, power, and admiration from others, they may deteriorate.

THEY ARE VISIONARY LEADERS.

These leaders understand the significance of developing a vision that people can believe in. They can see the big picture and see things that aren't there yet, and they will try to find them.

ASPIRE TO BE ADMIRED

Such leaders want to be admired by both their peers and those who report to them. They usually have a large number of "fans" who adore them. They can attract friends and followers and will gain more with their verbal abilities and articulation.

Leaders with narcissistic tendencies have strong oratory skills and can deliver excellent speeches.

DON'T TAKE CRITICISM SERIOUSLY

The narcissistic leader is sensitive to criticism at all times. He will not tolerate any criticism of anything he has done well and will obsess over it indefinitely. They will not like the sight of people disagreeing with them, and they can be quite abrasive towards those who have a negative opinion of them.

THEY DON'T PAY ATTENTION

Don't expect the leader to listen to or act on anything you say. They are so disinterested that they simply develop a defense mechanism to keep them from appreciating the criticism.

They also believe that those below them have little to offer and do not take their opinions seriously.

ARE RELIABLE

A leader with a healthy level of narcissism will have a set of values that they adhere to. They will keep moving along the path and will always try to make their plans work. When you have a leader who has toxic narcissism, you will notice that they have no values, are easily bored, and will change direction.

EMPIRE MINDSET

The narcissist in a position of power wishes to rule the world.

He wishes to leave a legacy that no one will question. He will go to any length to broaden his sphere of influence, hire more people so that he has more people to work with and increase his social standing.

If he is the CEO, he will always try to build another company after another to demonstrate his power.

EMPATHY DEFICIT

The narcissist leader will crave empathy and understanding from others, but they will be unable to provide the same to you. When there is a lot of chaos and radical change, a lack of empathy can be a strong point because they won't be bogged down by employee feelings, demands, and emotions.

EXTREMELY COMPETITIVE

The leader is a fierce competitor who is always looking for victory and growth. They take their roles seriously and see them as a way to put their survival skills and strength to the test.

They take advantage of others.

Leaders with narcissistic tendencies frequently try to exploit others for their benefit. They try to take advantage of others to achieve their goals. This could include limiting breaks, increasing work hours, and requiring immediate action.

Exploitation saps motivation and productivity. The employee may initially believe that the leader is charismatic, but this eventually backfires on them.

BUSINESS NARCISSISTS

You will almost certainly come into contact with a narcissist while doing business. When you do, you will immediately notice that this person has a disorder. Consider the characteristics of such a person in business.

THEY DEMONSTRATE THAT THEY KNOW EVERYTHING.

They will not hesitate to inform you about the country's laws or doctors about medicine. They believe they know everything there is to know about anything, even more than specialists in the field. They're not afraid to show it.

They will begin by stating facts, then argue and inform you about whatever you have brought up. They are even more knowledgeable about the company than the owners. They never back down from an argument and will seize any opportunity to educate you on their way of life and thinking.

THEY DO NOT FOLLOW THE RULES.

You've seen them - they jump lines like it's no big deal and put on a show that tells you they're important. They have no patience with the rules that you have established in your business.

They will also attempt to manipulate others so that they will break the rules on their behalf. They will constantly seek loopholes in the rules to demonstrate to you and others that they are far beyond your "stupid rules."

THEY WANT TO APPEAR SUPERIOR.

They want other people to notice something about their image. They will want to appear wealthy and well-liked. They will inquire about vehicles that they cannot afford. They'll ask you about items they know look good on them, and they'll make sure everyone hears them make the purchase.

They will seek out friends who are popular and famous to feel important.

They will boast about how great they are, while also implying that others are less intelligent or likable than them and inexperienced No matter how much training the individual has, the narcissist will try to demonstrate that they are the best at everything they do – better than anyone else.

MAKE AN EXCELLENT FIRST IMPRESSION

They have charming personalities, but you will quickly tire of them when you realize they have nothing to offer you.

They will appear to be very confident, enduring, and exciting, but you will soon discover what drives people away from them.

THEY BELIEVE THAT EVERYONE ADORES THEM.

They believe that they are held in high regard by everyone. They believe that if you aren't in their good graces, you must be envious of them and their accomplishments. They frequently attempt to punish anyone who expresses dissatisfaction.

Chapter 8

THE LONG-TERM EFFECTS OF NARCISSISTIC ABUSE

When you leave a narcissistic relationship, you may believe that everything is over and that you no longer have to suffer – but this may not be the case because things will happen that you will not believe.

When you believe you have moved on and have everything you need to make your life good and easy, the pieces of the relationship will begin to resurface. You thought you shattered them when you left the narcissist, but you realize they survived and continue to haunt you.

Things that happen to you in a relationship with a narcissist will stick with you for a long time until you seek therapy.

Consider the following effects:

1. THE MEMORIES WILL NOT DISAPPEAR

It's not your fault, but you'll start triggering memories that have been buried deep beneath the surface, and these memories will appear when the time is right.

An object, a location, or anything else that will cause you to remember things that you should have buried in the past will trigger the memories.

When this happens, you must recognize that it is not your fault, but rather the result of events that occurred while you were in the relationship. Consider these triggers as opportunities to communicate and grow.

THE DIFFICULTY OF RELIVING MEMORIES

Dwelling on the negative cause's mental problems. According to studies, the more you think about the issues that you encountered, the better through, the mistakes you made, the issues you encountered

The more you experience, the more likely you are to suffer from post-traumatic stress disorder, depression, and anxiety.

Mental illnesses last longer. The more you focus on problems, the more difficult it is to recover your mental health after an abusive relationship.

The memories combine to form bad habits over time. It will be difficult for you to change your way of thinking about various issues.

HOW TO STOP RELIVING TRAUMATIC MEMORIES

Know when it occurs. The more you dwell on the past, the more likely you are to become trapped in a negative cycle that is difficult to break free from. You must become aware of your habits and pay close attention to the times when you replay painful events in your mind. The sooner you notice the problem, the sooner you can choose to think about something more productive.

Find a workable solution. Thinking about what happened isn't very useful unless you're looking for a solution. Look for a way to handle the situation so that you don't have to relive the same memories. Try to learn from your mistakes and solve problems so you can move forward.

Think. The brain requires time to process what you're going through and come up with a solution. You can set aside a few minutes each day to think, reflect, and relax. Make this time a part of your daily routine.

Find a distraction. Find something to keep you occupied. You must be aware of when these thoughts arise and then find something to divert your attention away from them.

Visit the gym. Call a friend and talk about something else or work on a project. You can also move around to alter the environment.

Exercise mindfulness. This is ideal for living in the present moment.

Try to be completely present at the moment and forget about the past for a while.

2. NAUSEA

When you are subjected to emotional abuse from a narcissist, your body adapts in such a way that you no longer feel anything.

You will not feel good or bad - you will feel nothing because you believe you are safer.

However, the trauma remains, and it bubbles to the surface now and then. When you recognize that the trauma is still present and that you are suffering, you can begin working toward self-healing and liberation.

When you have feelings bottled up inside you, the next logical step is to find a safe place where you can acknowledge the feelings and honor yourself. You need to get to a place where you don't have to deal with the pain of losing the relationship.

This, however, will take some time. You'll have to practice a lot more before you feel safe enough to feel anything.

3. DISSATISFACTION

The pain of loss is accompanied by resentment toward others. Your rage builds up to the point where you have angry outbursts at any time.

You will be resentful of anyone or anything who reminds you of your abusive relationship. You may need to vent your frustrations in some way. To relieve some of the pressure, you can engage in critical rants, caustic humor, or passive-aggressive behavior toward anyone who crosses your path.

Because you may not be able to punish the abuser, you will turn to others, which may provide you with temporary relief but will make you feel worse about yourself.

You may discover that you provoke someone to become angry to feel better. Because anger and resentment feel more natural to you, they are more real than the conversation you need to have with them as a human being.

4. SLEEP ISSUES

If you've had problems with memories during the day, the night won't be any better. Even when you go to bed at night, you may find yourself thinking about what the abuser did to you. The few minutes before bedtime are usually the best times to think about and reflect on what happened during the day, but you will find yourself thinking about what the abuser told you or reliving the painful scenes over and over.

When you are sleep deprived, you will have less energy to deal with the effects of abuse, and your mood and overall performance will suffer. When this happens, you become a target for more abuse, which will keep you awake all night when you desperately need to sleep.

Some people will be able to sleep, but the trauma will not go away when they sleep; rather, it will return. The brain will continue to want to process the data. And because you can't turn off your brain, you'll end up reliving the trauma over and over.

5. ABUSE OF SUBSTANCES

If you discover that your relationship has caused you more pain than happiness, many people turn to drugs to make themselves happy and help them forget what they have been through.

If you have been emotionally abused on multiple occasions, it is easy to become addicted to drugs to feel better.

When memories resurface in your mind, you will undoubtedly seek release in other ways, the most common of which is drug abuse.

6. YOU HAVE TRUST PROBLEMS

When abuse takes root and undermines your self-worth and confidence, you are less likely to trust others because you are unsure if they will love you back. You are unsure that people will accept you as you are, and you will begin to question whom to trust and who not to trust.

This motivates you to seek out new ways to gain the approval of those around you and those whose opinions matter to you. You will pay more attention to how you look so that you can look your best.

best. You will also go out of your way to impress others so that they will love you.

You will discover that you try so hard to please people that you become obsessed with accomplishing things to look good in their eyes.

7. YOU PERFORM POORLY.

When you let the abuser get to you, your performance suffers at work, school, or at home. This is because you allowed feelings of low self-worth to interfere with your efforts.

When you believe that you aren't good enough or that you cannot do anything, you will end up living up to a low standard. You may also underperform to retaliate against the abuser.

When your spouse expects you to do something, you may only do it half-heartedly or not at all. If they criticize your appearance, you may avoid dressing well and stop caring about your appearance.

When you don't feel appreciated or worthy, it's difficult to act positively.

If you give your all and the reward isn't there or isn't fair, you'll find yourself slacking off.

8TH. SELF-HARM THOUGHTS

When you are frequently criticized by the person you love, your spirits will suffer. When this continues for an extended period, you will notice that you have progressed beyond the feeling of momentary sadness and will begin to feel sick - mentally, physically, and emotionally.

The accumulation of the actions and abuses of the person you love will lead to toxicity and negative self-talk, which will be difficult to overcome. Even if your abuser is no longer in the picture, you will replay some memories that you kept with you when the abuser was a part of you.

9. A SENSE OF SHAME

When you are under someone's control, you will lack confidence in making decisions, which can lead to feelings of shame.

When someone constantly attempts to bring you down, you will lose self-esteem and feel guilty knowing that you have messed up when, in reality, you haven't done anything wrong.

TEN. WITHHOLDING

When you are in an abusive relationship, the abuser will try to isolate you so that no one will notice when things are going wrong.

If the abuser convinces you to isolate yourself, fewer people will be aware of what is going on in the relationship. This habit becomes ingrained in you, and you will go about your life keeping secrets from the people who are important to you.

11. INABILITY TO BE INTIMATE

This phenomenon is difficult to explain, but it reaches a point where you don't want to be touched by anyone else.

Many survivors will feel this pain, and they will have no idea why. When someone touches them, they don't feel right, and they push people away. They must devote the necessary time to mastering this sensation.

12. INSECURITIES TAKE FORM

When you have previously been hurt, your insecurities become real. You are no longer required to act through them. When this happens, you should try to communicate your thoughts or encourage yourself to be honest.

POST-NARCISSISTIC STRESS DISORDER (PNSD)

This is a condition that develops after you have lived with and been subjected to the narcissist's extreme abuse. Let us examine the symptoms of this disorder.

AVOIDANCE

The primary symptom of this disorder is avoidance. The individual will avoid activities where they know they will encounter other people. They'll also avoid some previous relationships, locations, and situations.

The individual will also avoid thinking about or talking about the narcissist. By avoiding such people and situations, you will end up disrupting various aspects of your life, such as maintaining close relationships with people or even building one.

EXTREME ANXIETY

This condition can cause a great deal of anxiety. You will suffer from paranoia, panic attacks, and low self-esteem. When you have low self-esteem, you will begin to doubt your worth, which will cause you to struggle with simple daily tasks.

You will find it difficult to meet new people because you will begin to doubt their motives.

EMOTIONAL DEFICIENCY

When you've been through a lot of things that have rendered you emotionless, you'll have no emotion for anything that comes your way in life. When you begin to feel numb to everything, you will realize that you are experiencing isolation or emptiness. Typically, the sensation stems from depression and anxiety.

MEMORIES OF SUFFERING

This condition typically brings back painful memories, making you feel as if you are reliving them. You will relive the abusive event repeatedly.

Negative memories can be detrimental to your personal and professional life.

SELF-ESTEEM ISSUES

When they fail to meet the high standards, they have set for themselves, many people feel bad. This condition is the result of long-term suffering to which they have been subjected.

THEY ARE ALMOST ALWAYS LONELY.

When you have been abused by a narcissist, you will most likely begin to feel isolated all of the time. Even if you have the narcissist in your home, eating with them, living with them, and sleeping in bed with them, you will still feel alone.

You'll always find yourself curled up in a fetal position, wishing for someone to come over and simply wrap their arms around you to help you let go of the isolation and loneliness you're experiencing.

The main reason you feel empty and lonely is that you are living with someone you thought was real but was only pretending to make you fall in love with them. The person does not exist in any way, and they will abandon you at any time.

You will have the impression that the person simply tolerates you and only comes to you when they require something from you. If you are communicating with them but feel as if they are not hearing you, you are experiencing a mirage.

Remember that someone who loves you will want to spend a lot of time with you, learn more about you, and make sure you are safe and well cared for.

YOU'RE NOT FEELING WELL.

Even if you have a successful career and a solid foundation for your life, you will discover that you lack the necessary qualities to be happy. You have so many accomplishments, but when you think about them, you feel depressed and don't understand why you have them in the first place.

No matter how much the rest of the world notices and appreciates your accomplishments, the narcissist is blind to them and constantly mocks you for being so successful.

The narcissist will mock and ridicule you to appear superior to you. The goal is for you to lose your self-esteem and feel as low as they do.

They want to keep you under their control, so they will make it appear as if they are much better than you and have what it takes to accomplish more than you have so far.

When you receive this type of treatment, you will become dysfunctional and broken, losing everything, including your sense of worthiness.

You are living with a narcissist if you notice that you have become insignificant in your relationship and have failed in life in general.

YOU HAVE LOST YOUR IDENTITY.

The narcissist's trademark is that he will hijack and take over your world. They will try to consume your entire day, leaving you longing for some breathing room. You will notice the engulfment in the way they text, call, and even come to your workplace several times per day.

You will receive hundreds of emails and text messages, all designed to disrupt your day. They will encourage you to cut ties with your friends and even with your family. They'll want to tell you how to dress and what to eat, and they'll make sure you don't tell anyone about what's going on in your life.

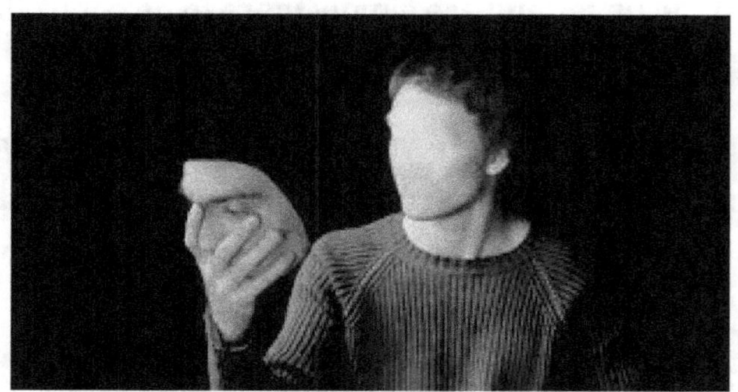

You live your life on eggshells, filled with anxiety at the prospect of doing something that will irritate the narcissist. So, before you do anything, you must first consider whether it will irritate the narcissist.

When you get past the relationship, you notice that you keep doing the same thing in every situation. You are constantly anxious and afraid, so anything you want to do takes longer than expected.

You must understand that a healthy relationship should not make you feel like a slave to another person. Instead, you must be free to perform at your best.

YOU HAVE LOST YOUR VALUES AND YOUR INTEGRITY.

As the abuse continues, you lose your values and begin to tolerate some of the things that made you uncomfortable because you believe you are in love.

If you previously stood up for your values and what you believed in, there will come a time when you don't know what values to stand up for and are simply there to be controlled and manipulated.

You begin to concentrate your efforts on how to persuade them to love you and treat you as the soul mate they claimed you were. Even though you now know the truth, you continue to believe their lies.

You find yourself doing crazy things "in the name of love," and you're not sure what got into you.

Chapter 9

THE SEVEN STEPS TO RECOVERY

Recovery from a narcissistic relationship can be extremely difficult. It usually takes longer than one would like, but it is the best way out of anger and bitterness. It can be a long stretch because it requires a very deliberate plan.

Recovery is often difficult and difficult because it completely changes your perception and thoughts about someone you thought you knew well or were close to. It always begins with accepting that even your favorite people can hurt you, and it is not your fault.

When you've confirmed that you've been abused, there's always that period where you wonder if detaching is the right decision, and you wonder if you're making a mistake because of the change in the things you're used to. This is completely normal and a necessary part of the healing process. The only thing you should remember is to not give in to your doubts.

There are various methods for healing from abuse that vary from person to person. However, some universal factors can be applied to any type of relationship.

7 RECOVERY STEPS

1. THERE IS NO CONTACT.

This is the first step toward healing that a victim of narcissistic abuse must take. Remove all contact with the abuser (s). This can be difficult at first because one is naturally drawn toward their abuser in the early stages of recovery.

You must convince yourself that you do not require the person in your life and embark on the road to recovery and healing.

No physical contact: Being in the same environment as the abuser will trigger memories of the abuse, which will have an impact on your daily life. Do it if it means moving away or changing jobs. It helps to gradually clear those thoughts from your mind, and with time, you realize you can live without your abuser.

Narcissists also know how to manipulate their victims, and physical contact only adds to this.

No emotional contact: This is the most difficult, as you must constantly remind yourself that you do not need to be in touch or have a relationship with the abuser. Also, train your mind to move forward and even build better relationships. Things start to get better and more positive once you can control your emotions and realize you don't need the abuser in your life.

When you have completely cut off all links and contact, you can consider personal healing, which is a separate process in and of itself.

2. CONSIDER THE SITUATION CALMLY.

Do not rush to move on or attempt to forget the experience you have had. You must go back and calmly process what happened and the various events that led to one thing leading to another.

Start thinking about why you left rather than how you left, focusing on how their actions made you feel. This will help you accept the fact that you had to leave for your good.

When you think deeply about your feelings and step back from them, you will notice that things begin to make sense and you will realize that you require better. You realize that severing ties with the abuser are in your best interests and the best way forward. This is also the time to recognize that whatever was done to you was not your fault and was the result of someone else's negative behavior. You can choose to write down and highlight the red flags you may have ignored that led you to become involved in the abuse, as well as how to spot them in the future. This always aids in better digesting events and situations making the same decision not to be caught in the same situation again

After such experiences, victims may seek sympathy from others or attend a pity party. They fall into a cycle of self-pity and personal criticism, which only serves to aggravate their pain and make them feel worthless. Cut yourself some slack and recognize that you are deserving of better.

Don't pass judgment on yourself: Do not berate yourself harshly for being duped by the abuser's lies and charm. Most of the time, you may feel guilty for falling for their tricks, but don't be too hard on yourself. Recognize that it could happen to anyone and be grateful that you could finally see things as they were.

When you are gentle with yourself, it is easier to work on your emotions and create space for healing. When you constantly judge yourself harshly, you will keep reliving those negative experiences, which will only delay your progress and recovery.

One event does not define your life: Just because you had a bad experience that lasted a while doesn't mean your entire life is a shambles. This means that an abusive relationship should not be used to conclude that you have a bad life.

Recognize that it was only a small part of your life and begin making positive memories. Many people are so focused on a single experience that they forget they have a whole life ahead of them. Do not let this happen to you.

Don't let your pain define you: Pain is unpleasant, but it can also be beneficial. Pain enables us to learn and make sound decisions. It also makes us conscious of our human emotions and limitations. Do not allow your pain to define your identity. This entails constantly whining and complaining about everything that has occurred. Work on being a more positive person by reminding yourself that you are valuable and important. Know that the pain was a stage in your life that helped you move from one stage to another and learn from it When we let pain define us, we miss out on other wonderful experiences in life. To fully recover from such events, you must understand that pain is a natural part of life. There will be rainy days, but that does not mean that the sunny days are unimportant.

When you are compassionate with yourself, you can easily embrace your experiences and forge a path forward. It also makes you appreciate the good things in life and allows you to focus on improving.

4. PERSONALIZE RATHER THAN GENERALIZE

We sometimes generalize experiences without realizing that everyone is defined by their unique personality. As an example, suppose a man cheats on a woman and she concludes that all men cheat. This should never happen because one person should never lead you to conclude an entire group. If your mother abused you, don't blame all your parents for your bad experience.

Everyone deserves to be judged for who they are, not for what they did. This will help you build even more healthy relationships because you will understand that having one bad relationship with someone should not prevent you from having other healthy ones.

Personalizing a behavior to the specific person who has hurt you allows you to see life in a more positive light.

A single bad apple should not necessarily determine the fate of the entire crop. This is an attitude that must be fostered to avoid prolonged bitterness in one's life, as they are prone to seeing so many things through the same lens as the abuser.

5. ACCEPT PERSONAL RESPONSIBILITY FOR YOUR HEALING

The person who suffers the most is you, the abused, and because this is a personal issue, it is up to you to take charge, heal, and recover. You are the most familiar with yourself, where you have been, and what you have been through. You are aware of your strengths and weaknesses. If you focus your thoughts on what the abuser has projected onto you, you will undoubtedly become that person.

Begin by knowing who you are and mentally stamping that identity. Continue to remind yourself of the good person you are and make that your daily mantra. Understand that you can only be as good as you believe you are. Be deliberate in your healing, knowing that even minor triggers can send you back to your bitterness. You can begin with:

Consultation with a professional counselor: A problem that is shared is a problem that is half solved. If you are comfortable speaking with a specialist, do so. It may not change what happened to you, but it will help you deal with your emotions and may help you recover from some of the trauma.

Immersion in your hobbies: Do you have any hobbies that you could pursue? This is always beneficial because it allows you to channel your energy into something positive. It keeps you motivated and gives you something to look forward to, which is exactly what we need when we're feeling overwhelmed. Get things going, and you'll notice that the burden of the abuse has worn off over time.

Accepting a new challenge: Begin reading a book, enroll in a dance class, or enroll in cooking classes. You require some form of therapy at this point, and it can be made easier by engaging in mind-expanding activities. This will introduce you to new interests and keep your mind occupied. It helps you get rid of some things and is also beneficial to your mental health, which is the most important goal.

Taking your time before starting a new relationship: Another mistake some people make is entering new relationships after leaving an abusive situation.

Before getting groovy with someone new, make sure you're completely healed. This gives you time to put things into perspective, and you are less likely to make mistakes. When you enter a relationship with a wounded heart, you are bound to be judgmental and will unknowingly hurt that other person.

6. FORGIVENESS

This is the most important part. You must forgive both your abuser and yourself. You will not be able to heal unless you forgive. Forgive and remember that there is more to life and that it was just another experience, so life must go on. Take whatever time it takes to get it off your chest and, if possible, seek closure. If it is a family member, REACH OUT WHEN YOU ARE COMFORTABLE and let them know you have forgiven them. It is not an easy task, but it is worthwhile. Without forgiveness, you will always harbor a grudge against the other person and will always associate certain events with what you have gone through. Forgiving gives you a new perspective and allows you to see things differently.

7. MAKE CERTAIN YOU ARE NEVER ABUSED AGAIN.

Remember that once you've forgiven and received a clean bill of health and recovery, you should never go through a similar situation again. Know the red flags and how to spot them to avoid ending up in the same painful situation again. Set a high standard for yourself, knowing that you deserve the best, and put an end to any abusive behavior. When given a second chance, it only makes sense to exercise greater caution when dealing with the same issues.

Healing from an abusive, narcissistic relationship is not easy, and the individual must put in a lot of effort to be completely healed. It does not rule out the possibility; it simply necessitates more effort than usual. When you reach that point of total healing, you begin to appreciate what you would have gone through and make the best of it.

Conclusion

Relationships are supposed to be enjoyable and exciting. You are two people from different backgrounds who have come together to form an unbreakable bond.

- The narcissist then enters the picture.
- This is someone who tries to make you appear irrelevant in every way.
- Being in a relationship with a narcissist can be aggravating and depressing.

WHAT IS IT?

Narcissism is a personality trait that everyone possesses to some extent. Some people have them at excessively high levels, while others have them at the bare minimum. It, like any other trait in the world, exists on a spectrum, and everyone falls somewhere along it.

- Being a narcissist isn't all bad; in fact, having some of the traits can be beneficial at times.
- It becomes problematic when it reaches a pathological level.
- When you have a high level of narcissism, you are diagnosed with NPD.

SOCIETY'S NARCISSISTS

In our society, the condition has become all too common. Narcissists are now found in love relationships, boardrooms, political positions, homes, and even religious institutions. It's become a common occurrence, and everyone is bearing the brunt of it.

They're everywhere, and the worst part is that you might be sharing a bed with one and have no idea if they're narcissists or not. You must understand what makes them tick and recognize the signs that you are in a relationship with one.

Signs You're in a Relationship with a Narcissist

The good news is that a narcissist can be easily identified when you see one. This is because you will notice signs that the person has NPD. Here are a few indicators:

They have a regal air about them. The narcissist will brag about how wonderful they are. They will exaggerate their accomplishments to demonstrate that they are always better than you. They tell you all of this because they expect you to treat them as your superior, even though the facts show that they have nothing to show for it.

They will brag about how great they are and how they can help you improve if you work with them. They will claim that they have connections in high places and that they can get anything they want without having to work for it.

They believe they are entitled to far more than the world has to offer. They will denigrate their family and then talk about how they came from a poor background and worked hard to ensure their success. You will be bombarded with promises about how they can get you out of your rut and make you famous.

They were initially quite charming. They told you how much they loved you and sent you messages and emails all the time, even making you fall in love with them. They will lavish you with praise after praise, making you feel loved and giving you all the attention, you desire. They will, however, turn against you if you do something that disappoints them.

They dominate the conversation. If you've noticed that the person always dominates the conversation, you should be aware that you're in love with a narcissist. They do everything they can to stay ahead of you in terms of stories. They will fabricate a story to make you look bad. They do this because they believe they are always superior to others and that what you say isn't as important as what they must do.

They also do this because it makes them feel more confident.

They have no empathy. When you tell them you have a problem, they won't believe you, and they may even turn it against you and make it their own if they notice how much attention it is getting. They do not recognize any of your emotions. They don't care if you've had a bad day or if you've had a disagreement with someone else; all they want is to talk about them.

The good news is that you won't have to deal with all of the narcissist's issues. You have a method for dealing with them that makes it simple for you.

HOW TO DEAL WITH A NARCISSIST

There are various types of narcissists, and you must understand how to deal with them. Here are a few pointers to help you get started.

RECOGNIZE THEM

You must recognize narcissists for what they are. When you enter their lair and decide to fall for them, you may be perplexed by the charm that they exude. You might be drawn to them because of their lofty promises and grandiose ideas.

Before you fall for them, you should observe how they treat others and then determine who they truly are. This will help you deal with them effectively.

STOP FOCUSING ON THEM

When you live with a narcissist, you will take all of the attention and then give it to them. This will boost their ego and turn them into heroes. Take the time to try to shift the focus away from them and toward yourself or something else.

Remember that the more you focus on them, the bigger their ego grows.

SPEAK OUT

There are times when you simply ignore the person and remain silent. However, doing so gives them the energy to stress you out even more. What you should do is try to speak up and point out the various issues that concern you are facing so that they understand you are dissatisfied with what they are doing